The Puppy Primer

Patricia B. McConnell, Ph.D
and Brenda Scidmore

McConnell Publishing, Ltd. I Black Earth, WI

McConnell Publishing Ltd.
Black Earth, Wisconsin

Cover and internal design by jam graphics & design

ISBN # 1-891767-13-5

For information, go to
www.patriciamcconnell.com

9 8

To Lassie, always a puppy
and to
Kato, a guy with a great sense of humor

TABLE OF CONTENTS

INTRODUCTION

Good Puppy Owner! Goooood Puppy Owner! How clever of you to start now on your puppy's education! You should feel good because you are caring and committed enough to take responsibility for your new dog's welfare. As you know, there's more to your puppy's well-being than physical health; your dog's behavior will influence the quality of life of everyone in the family for years to come, whether they have two legs or four.

The Puppy Primer is designed as a six-week training program to start you and your puppy off on the right paw. Each chapter includes *Special Topics* (Housetraining and Crate Training for example), *New Exercises* (like the steps of Come, Sit and Down training) and *Practice Makes Perfect*, (the second or third steps of an exercise, so that your pup can begin to master the behavior.)

Inside this book you'll learn how to humanely and effectively teach your pup how to pay attention, to follow the "house rules" and to be a joy to live with. You'll learn how positive reinforcement makes training fast and fun. Along the way you'll expand your ability to teach your dog good habits (rather than just correcting bad ones), and manage the home environment such that it's easy for your puppy to do the right thing.

While your pup is maturing, remember, Lassies are made, not born. Your dog didn't come into the world with the ability to understand English or to know the social conventions of our culture. By the same token, you were not born instinctively knowing how to train a dog.

Dog training involves skills that anyone can learn, if they are willing to invest the time and energy. The person who trained the television star Lassie had to master those abilities just like the rest of us! We all start from the same place.

We are delighted that you chose to begin this journey with us! We hope that raising your pup involves the whole family—dog training works best if everyone is consistent in what is communicated. You'll get the most out of this book by reading it one chapter at a time and working for one week on the exercises in each chapter before moving on. However, don't hesitate to use the book in the way that works best for you—perhaps looking into a "special topic" that you'd like to know more about right away. Ideally, go through an exercise when you can get up right away and practice what you've read. Most importantly, have fun! Training can and should be equally fun for you and your dog—isn't that why you got a dog in the first place, to add happiness and joy to your life? So read on, and look forward to creating a great relationship with your new best friend.

[Note: Rather than calling your puppy an "it," or using the awkward "s/he," we have elected to alternate between "he" and "she" in the text. We are grateful that there are only two sexes!]

1
FIRST THINGS FIRST

★ SPECIAL TOPICS

SOCIALIZATION

One of the most important things you can do to help your puppy grow up to be a friendly, confident, dog is to *socialize* your puppy now. Socialization, as the term is commonly used, means giving your pup careful, positive exposure to all of the things that he might encounter as an adult dog. In your pup's case, that includes other dogs and the full range of people that he might encounter, from young, bouncy children to someone in a wheelchair. Depending on your circumstances, you might add cats, horses, birds or ferrets to the list.

If a puppy isn't exposed to a variety of people and dogs when young, he might not be friendly or confident with them as an adult. Fear in puppies is often exhibited as aggression in adult dogs, so now is the time to create positive experiences with individuals outside of the family. However, take note of the "how to" information below: socialization incorrectly done (which is regrettably a common practice) can cause more harm than good.

ENVIRONMENTAL STIMULATION Your pup also needs to experience a range of environments, from rides in the car, visits to neighbors, and walks in the country. This type of *environmental stimulation* can actually change the way your pup's brain is structured, and allows him to be more flexible about changes when he's grown up. Dogs who have had limited exposure to a variety of environments are more likely to be stressed when you move, go on vacation or add to the family, so it's important to take this aspect of raising your puppy seriously. Of course, there is also a genetic aspect to your dog's responses, but it's always a good idea to do what you can to help him grow up to be well adjusted by exposing him to positive experiences in a range of environments.

To accomplish this, take your pup out and about without taking her places where she'll be scared by too much activity or noise. Teach her to ride in the car, to visit the vet's office (a great place to give treats in the lobby and then drive home!) or to the groomer's shop. Visit a friend's house, go camping and explore the woods, or sleep out in a friend's backyard tent. Let your puppy walk on shiny floors, grass, pavement, dirt and gravel. In general, go to a wide variety of places, but again, be sure not to take her to places where she might get overwhelmed by too much noise or movement.

WHEN TO SOCIALIZE YOUR PUP Now is the right time! A puppy's brain is not fully formed until the age of five months. However, there is a "critical" or "sensitive" period of socialization from 3 to 12-14 weeks of age that is especially important. This is the age range in which pups are most influenced by meeting potential "members of the pack."

Our experience suggests that social interactions continue to be especially important during the first year of a dog's life, especially during the "sensitive" period mentioned above and in early adolescence (5-9 months in most dogs). Guard against stopping socialization too early: it's not good enough to have lots of company the first weeks of your dog's life, and then live the life of a hermit for the next year. Socialization and environmental stimulation are ongoing processes. Ideally, positive social encounters should continue throughout your dog's life, so you should never stop "socializing," but pay special attention to it in the early stages of your dog's development when it can do the most good.

HOW TO SOCIALIZE YOUR NEW DOG The most important thing to keep in mind is that you are conditioning your dog to enjoy strangers, other dogs and new environments. That means it is up to you to manage the situation so that your pup is not overwhelmed or traumatized. The most common mistake that owners make is to "socialize" their dog by taking him into an environment that is simply too frightening. A "sensitive" period in your puppy's life means just that, and negative experiences can have just as profound an effect as positive ones.

That's why you'll want to take your pup to safe places that will stimulate him but not overwhelm him. Young pups, even those who are older than 14 weeks, should be exposed to positive interactions with people, other dogs or new environments several times a week. Keep in mind that puppies need to be exposed to many different people in order to generalize the concept that, overall, people are okay. However, don't try to force things. At first, limit introductions to one or two strangers at a time and avoid crowds. If your dog looks a bit fearful, with a closed mouth and rounded eyes, or is flicking his tongue out, yawning, or turning away to avoid contact, ask others to stand still and let your pup come to them. Avoid letting him become overwhelmed by people looming over him or picking him up. Have strangers toss treats for a shy puppy, so that he learns to associate new people with good things, rather than being frightened.

Young puppies, even those who are older than 14 weeks, should be exposed to positive interactions with people and other dogs.

The same holds true for encounters with children—a dog may be comfortable around the kids in his own household, but if he's never had a good experience with children outside of the "pack," he might grow up to be nervous around the neighborhood kids. Children look, sound, and move differently than adults, and they tend to make more sudden and erratic movements.

In addition, young children are often unaware that they are scaring or hurting a young dog. It is your job to protect your pup so that he doesn't learn he has to protect himself. Quietly intervene when children try to pick up your puppy (which is frightening to most dogs) and go out of your way to help the children interact in a positive way (see Chapter 5 for more on children and dogs). Limit the time that visiting children are allowed to play with your pup; young dogs need lots of naps and can get grumpy or stressed just like overly tired children. Teach the kids to ask your puppy to perform a simple trick, and ask them to give the pup a treat when he does. Most importantly, observe your puppy carefully for signs of anxiety or fear, and be thoughtful about how much "newness" he can tolerate.

SOCIALIZING WITH OTHER DOGS Young dogs need to learn that being approached by unfamiliar dogs is a fun experience, not an overwhelming or scary one. For that reason, avoid taking your pup to a dog park or a puppy class in which all the pups are thrown together into a canine mosh pit. Being mobbed by multiple dogs is not socialization, it's a potentially traumatic experience that can cause your dog trouble later on. It is best to set up play sessions between your pup and a few other dogs at a time, at first keeping the group to a total of two or three dogs. Gradually increase the numbers if you know that the other dogs have good social skills. Puppy classes are excellent IF the trainers divide the room into smaller areas and let pups of similar size and temperaments play with each other. On the other hand, throwing a 10 week-old Yorkie puppy into a group of five-month old Labradors is a great way to create a dog-dog aggression problem down the road as the Yorkie matures. Pups who are frightened early in life may become defensively aggressive if they feel they are in danger from something that scared them, even if it happened years in the past.

Don't be fooled into thinking that because you own other dogs your puppy will be well socialized. Your pup needs to meet dogs that are initially *unfamiliar* to him, and needs to interact with them in order to learn all the rules of polite canine-to-canine encounters. Whenever possible, your pup should also meet various different types of dogs: tall ones, tiny ones, fat ones, ones with floppy ears, ones that snort or breathe loudly…you get the idea! Interactions should all be with friendly dogs so your pup has lots of positive experiences and learns to trust other dogs, not to be frightened of them. Puppies learn a lot about how to "play well with others" when they are young, so do what you can to allow your pup to play with other dogs, as long as they are polite and well-socialized themselves.

HEALTH CONCERNS? You should know that there is some risk of disease transmission when young puppies are exposed to the world at large before they've been fully vaccinated. Most pups have not completed their series of vaccinations until about 16 weeks of age, but the critical period of socialization ends around 12–14 weeks. If you wait until your pup is fully vaccinated, you risk inadequate socialization; but if you take your pup out and about, you risk your puppy catching an infectious disease. It's a balancing act that every owner has to handle depending on their circumstances and their comfort level. We recommend utilizing areas like responsible puppy classes where all the dogs have had at least one or two shots, and the houses of friends with fully vaccinated dogs. Avoid areas in which you don't know if other dogs have been vaccinated (like dog parks). In over twenty years, we've seen very few cases of healthy puppies catching a disease from other dogs, but hundreds of examples of dogs with serious behavioral problems related to inadequate or improper socialization. Please talk to your veterinarian about ways to cut the risks, while still taking advantage of this sensitive period of socialization.

> *Positive reinforcement is the key to efficient and effective training.*

POSITIVE REINFORCEMENT

Now is the time to use positive reinforcement to teach your pup that she'll feel good if she does what you ask. Don't be fooled by arguments that dogs only do what you say because you are "dominant" over them. "Dominance," just like "social status" in human society, is only relevant a small percentage of the time, and has nothing to do with coming when called or not jumping up on visitors. Besides, who wants a relationship based on a power differential instead of love and mutual cooperation? Luckily for us (and our dogs), positive reinforcement is efficient and effective at teaching our dogs what we want them to do. It leads to highly reliable responses and makes training fun for all involved. What's not to like?

Here's what you need to remember:

• Positive reinforcement is defined by your dog: it's whatever makes your dog more likely to repeat a behavior. For most dogs, that includes a small but tasty treat (like cut up meat, cheese or high quality commercial training treats), play with a favorite toy, or praise and petting IF done in a way that your pup truly enjoys.

• Timing is crucial: If you give your dog a treat for sitting at your feet after she's come when called, you've just reinforced sitting, not for coming when called. Give your dog a treat, *immediately* upon completion of the behavior you wanted.

MAKE PRAISE MEANINGFUL TO YOUR DOG Teach your pup to associate praise or the sound of a clicker (both are "secondary reinforcers;" see Chapter 3 for more on clicker training) with treats that your dog absolutely adores. Until you pair praise or a click with treats, they are both meaningless noises to your dog. Say "Good Dog!" or click the clicker, then follow immediately with a small but tasty treat. With repetition your dog will begin to associate the sounds you are making with feeling good. She'll be excited to hear the words or the clicking noise, and will begin to "work" to try to get you to make those noises again! Handheld clickers are an especially precise way to signal to a dog that she just did something wonderful. The next section describes a great way to practice using treats to get your dog's attention.

 # NEW EXERCISES

ATTENTION

We all want dogs who love us completely . . . and also do whatever we say whenever we say it! Not much to ask, hey? But the first part of "obedience" is attention—your dog can't listen and respond if you don't have his attention. However, you're competing against a distracting environment, from the sight of the dog next door to the smell of chipmunks in the grass. That's why the following exercise is so important; it is designed to teach your dog that it pays to offer you his attention, because you are the most interesting game in town. In some ways, it is the easiest training you'll ever do.

I'M WORTH IT! Put your dog on a leash, and go outside to an area with mild to moderate distractions. Give your dog a tiny, tasty treat every time he happens, all on his own, to look in your direction. (Be sure to have the treats easily accessible, but don't show them to your dog before you start.) Avoid calling his name or trying to get him to look at you, just wait for the brief moment in which his head turns toward you, praise, and immediately pop a treat in his mouth. Your only job is to keep at least part of your attention on your dog, so that you notice the times he looks at you. This can be harder than it sounds: It turns out we're not always so good at paying attention either! However, it's well worth the trouble. The more attention you get from your dog, the more chances you'll have to influence his behavior.

These hints will make this exercise most worthwhile:
• Don't "cheat" by trying to get his attention! The idea here is to let him initiate the activity, not to teach him to respond to something that you are doing. If he doesn't glance your way within a minute or two, move forward a few steps, and be ready to praise and treat the microsecond he looks in your direction.

• As opposed to other training exercises, it's okay to start in an area with some distractions. Just don't take him somewhere so distracting that he'll never turn to look at you no matter how long you're there.

• Patience is a virtue! Give him a minute or two to look in your direction (and be ready!), but if he looks completely absorbed in sights and scents, move to a less distracting environment.

• Try this in short sessions (3 to 5 minutes are plenty), several times a day if you can. Once you've given him five to ten treats, end the session.

TEACHING SIT

Here's an exercise that helps you practice your timing, learn an effective training method and get your pup started sitting when asked. Using this method, you'll LURE your dog into the position you want, and then REWARD her response. We've found that the lure/reward method is the fastest way to teach actions like Sit, Down and Stand. Here's what it looks like when teaching your pup to sit on cue (after all, she already knows how to sit by herself, it's doing it when you ask that takes training!):

HELP HER GET IT RIGHT Start out with few or no distractions; puppies learn best when they can concentrate on a new task. If you're at home, start inside in a quiet room. If you're in a puppy class, move your pup away from the other dogs as best you can, and get her attention by giving her some extra yummy treats.

Put a small, tasty treat (about the size of a pea) between your thumb and forefinger, and squat down in front of your pup. Hold the treat about an inch away from her nose, and let her get a good whiff of it. Once you have her undivided attention, slowly move your hand back over her head, between her ears and toward her tail. Don't move your hand up—if you do she might jump up to try to get it. Keep the treat close to the outline of your dog's head as you move it back toward her tail. If you move at the correct speed, she'll try to follow the scent with her nose, which tilts her head up and her rump down. If she stops following the treat, just move it back to her nose and start again. Notice that at this point you're not saying anything, just moving a treat to lure her into position

In most cases, your pup will end up with her rump on the floor in a sitting position, and you can immediately praise her brilliance and pop the treat in her mouth. Let her get up again, then repeat two or three times. Don't over do this—she's just a pup after all, and doesn't have a long attention span.

TROUBLE SHOOTING If your pup hasn't read the books and just backs up but doesn't sit, try the same method in a corner, where she can't back up at all. Just stay quiet and calm, no hurry here, and be ready to praise and treat the instant her little bottom hits the ground.

Once you can reliably get her to sit by moving the treat between her ears and toward her tail, start to precede your movement with the word "Sit." Be sure to say the word a tiny bit before you move your hand—in later weeks we'll work on dropping out the hand movement altogether. However, for now, she's learning both a visual cue and an acoustic one, and that will come in handy as she matures. It is also easier for dogs to learn visual signals than spoken ones, so you'll find it useful to have a movement that easily evolves into a hand signal in short order.

SIT AND DOWN TOGETHER; PUPPY PUSH UPS!

You can use the same lure/reward method to start teaching a "Down" cue. Begin with your pup in a sit, and move the food close to her nose again. This time move your hand down toward the floor, moving it slowly enough that your pup's nose follows the smell. Avoid moving your hand forward, away from your puppy, or she'll get up to follow it. Move your hand straight down or even slightly toward your dog's belly. Be patient here, this often takes a bit longer than luring a dog into a sitting posture.

If your pup won't go all the way down, put the treat back up to her nose and slowly move it downward again until your hand rests on the floor. Most pups will eventually lie down, and the instant they do, praise or click and give her the treat *while she is still lying down.*

TROUBLE SHOOTING If you are having trouble getting your pup to lie down, and you've varied the speed at which you move your hand and patiently waited for her to move the front half of her body toward the ground, don't give up! Try luring her under a chair or table (or your outstretched leg?) that requires your dog to lie down and crawl underneath it to get the treat. As soon as she lowers her forequarters, be ready to praise and treat. Then begin again, eventually treating her for lying all the way down on her way to the goodies. Once she'll do it easily with the prop, try it without it.

Word to the wise: don't ask your dog to lie down from a standing posture yet … that's harder for her, and will be appropriate in later weeks, but not when she is first getting started.

KEEP IT SHORT Practice sit and down in *very short* sessions throughout the day. Don't wait for dinnertime (every dog sits for his dinner bowl)—ask for a sit when walking from one room to the next, or practice sit and down during a commercial while watching television. Professional trainers know that the key to having a dog who listens anytime, anywhere, is to practice, well . .. . anytime, anywhere! Just be sure to keep sessions short, but make the cues relevant no matter where or when you use them.

★ SPECIAL TOPIC

HOUSETRAINING

Here's the good news: housetraining is a relatively simple concept to teach your puppy. It isn't rocket science, from either your perspective or your pup's. But here's the rub: successful housetraining takes planning and attention to detail. Once you've done it, it becomes second nature, but if it's been awhile since you trained your last dog, it requires a change in habits. If you concentrate on the details as you start this process, they will quickly become habitual, and eventually you won't even notice the effort. (Well, okay, not too much!)

THE BASICS
Your pup should be in one of three situations at all times during the learning phase of housetraining.

He should be either:

1. Outside, while you actively watch for and reinforce any urination or defecation.

2. Inside with your *constant* supervision.

3. Crated or gated off in a small, puppy-proofed room.

Here are more detailed descriptions of these three situations:

OUTSIDE WITH YOU Don't expect your pup to become house trained if you open the door, let him outside and don't watch to see if he goes or not. Pups get distracted and forget to potty—it's our job to ensure that they "go," and to reinforce them for it immediately.

Begin by taking him to the area designated as his toilet area. Sometimes it helps to take him out on a leash, even in a fenced backyard, to keep him focused on one spot. If you always take him to this same place, he will tend to seek it out in the future. Stand still and quietly wait until he looks ready to eliminate. As he squats, quietly say the cue you have chosen. ("Go Potty" is popular, but we like "Hurry Up," living as we do where it can be below freezing much of the year!) Wait quietly as he goes, and as soon as he is done, immediately praise him and hand him a tasty treat. The treat is crucial: you want him to think going potty outside is the best game in town. Do NOT stand at the door and give him a treat when he trots back to you—then he's getting the treat for coming back to the house, not for eliminating outside.

INSIDE WITH CONSTANT SUPERVISION This is the hard one! It means that you literally keep your eyes on your pup every second when he is loose in the house. It can help to either leash him to you or shut doors so that he can't leave the room. This is important: it only takes a few seconds for your pup to run into another room and urinate, and it's your job to prevent that from happening. Once he's pottied a few times in the house, it can become a habit, and, as we all know, it's a lot easier to create a good habit rather than trying to change a bad one.

Beware of those times when you are physically "there" with your pup, but functionally you are not! "Accidents" often happen when you are preoccupied with something else. You are the teacher, and therefore responsible for watching for those subtle signs that indicate that your pup may need to go outside.

CRATED OR GATED OFF IN A SMALL PUPPY-PROOF ROOM Pups are less inclined to potty in areas where they sleep or eat. A laundry room or a kitchen with a baby gate across the door can work well, but for many pups, a crate is an ideal place to nap, chew on a chew toy and learn to control their bladders.

Generally dogs will try their best not to soil their sleeping area, so your pup is unlikely to soil his crate. If he does have an occasional accident in it, don't worry about it, just clean it up well (see below) and try to figure out why it happened. Was he in there too long? Did you make sure he went outside before he went into his crate or room? Did you change his diet? A few accidents in the crate aren't a crisis, but if it continues, you need to sort the problem out and get it turned around. Talk to your vet and/or a trainer if you're having ongoing problems.

HELPFUL TIPS
• Take tasty treats with you when you go outside with your pup, and give him a treat immediately after he has eliminated. This is THE key to fast and efficient housetraining. Be sure it's a treat he really, really likes and that he gets it immediately after going potty. Does that mean you have to go outside with him all the time? Well, yes, at least for now, even in the snow and rain. But take heart, that won't last forever, and it's worth the trouble to have a fully housetrained dog for years to come.

The best way to housetrain your dog is to give treats immediately after he potties outside.

• Sorry, but you can't overdo it when it comes to how often you take your puppy outside to urinate or defecate! Pups haven't yet developed full bladder control until 20 or 30 weeks of age, (longer if your dog is a small breed), so they often need to urinate at least once every hour or so that they are awake, even more frequently if they are active. Take them out every half hour, or more frequently, while they are awake and active. As a general rule dogs tend to be more metabolically active first thing in the morning and again in the late afternoon to evening.

• If your pup doesn't eliminate while outside, watch him like a hawk when back inside (or put him in his crate), and take him out again in 10 to 15 minutes. Be aware that it's not uncommon for a pup to "go" outside, then come inside and need to "go" again 5 or 10 minutes later. In that case he probably didn't relieve himself completely the first time. Learn your dog's natural pattern, so you aren't taken by surprise once you go back into the house. (Honest, it's just physiological, he's not deliberately trying to make your life more difficult!)

• Remember that, just like us, dogs can wait much longer periods without needing to eliminate when they are sleeping. Don't make the mistake of thinking that because your pup can go all night without needing to "go," he can wait that long during waking periods. He can't. Young pups especially need to go a lot when active, and immediately after eating or drinking.

• Restrict your pup's access to rooms that you rarely use. Keep doors shut and use puppy gates to keep him confined to areas where you spend most of your time. This will prevent him from dashing away to relieve himself in a place he doesn't define as "home."

READING YOUR PUPPY'S SIGNALS Dogs frequently try to tell us when they need to potty—but just as often, we miss what they are trying to communicate. Do all you can to learn your puppy's signals that mean he is ready to relieve himself. You may have had a dog in the past who went to the door when he needed to potty, but most puppies haven't read that memo yet, so don't expect it! Besides, you shouldn't wait for him to "tell" you he wants to go out—it is your job to take him outside before he needs to go. However, it is also very helpful to translate "Oh boy, I really need to go" from canine to human!

Here is a list of circumstances and signals that may mean your puppy needs to urinate or defecate:

• Your pup just woke up.

• He got up from munching on a chew toy.

• He just ate or drank.

• You just greeted him and released him from confinement.

• He is wandering away from an area in which he was playing.

• He is sniffing the floor with his nose directly on the floor or carpet.

• He's circling while sniffing.

• He is looking a bit confused or distracted from what he was doing.

• He is looking in the direction of the door he usually goes out, or pacing or wandering into that area.

• He is wandering over to an area that he has soiled before, especially if he starts sniffing in that area.

• He was playing hard (especially if he was playing with another dog or a human) and he hasn't been out for a while. Sometimes pups can get so busy playing they just squat in mid-romp! Avoid this by interrupting hard, prolonged play session with potty breaks.

• You see him begin to squat. (Okay, that was obvious, but still . . .)

By now you must have decided that your puppy should be taken out every five minutes! It's not usually that bad, we promise, especially once you learn your pup's daily pattern.

OOPS! FOUND AN ACCIDENT!

What if you made a mistake? You got distracted, you turned your back for a moment, or for whatever reason you now find a "surprise" on your carpet? Well, if you didn't actually see the pup making the mess, it's too late to do anything about it now (except to clean it up). Don't rub your pup's nose in it, don't hit him, and don't give in to the urge to punish him in any other way. He won't understand why you're upset, and besides, it was you that gave him the opportunity to make a mistake, wasn't it? So don't blame the puppy! Instead, take a breath, put him in his crate, and clean it up.

If you do see your pup begin to squat in the house, make a loud, abrupt noise to startle him. (We avoid clapping since it is a great way to encourage your dog to come when called.) Something as simple as a slap on a nearby wall or table can be enough to startle and interrupt him. Then immediately rush him outside (cheerfully) and give him tons of praise and a treat for eliminating outdoors. Come back in, and put him in his crate for a moment while you clean up his accident.

Remember that the goal is to startle him to interrupt the behavior, not to punish him. Being very harsh with him or punishing the mistake will only teach him that he shouldn't potty while you are watching. So logically, being the intelligent chap that he is, next time he'll have enough sense to sneak off somewhere and do it while you aren't looking. What's more, he might not "go" when outside on walks anymore, because you are there, and he has learned that you get upset when he tries to relieve himself.

CLEANING UP How you clean up "accidents" in the house is crucial. If you don't remove the source of the odor completely, it will attract your dog back to the spot like a neon sign saying "Public Restroom—Potty Here!!"

Avoid bleach or household cleaners. Many cleaners contain ammonia, which will attract your dog back to that location, just like the scent of his own urine will. Instead use a commercial product designed especially for this purpose (like Nature's Miracle® or Outright®, or GetSerious®, to name just a few). Properly used, these products will remove the source of the odor so your pup won't be attracted to that particular spot again. In a pinch, you can use baking soda or club soda to neutralize portions of the odor.

TIME FOR MORE FREEDOM IN THE HOUSE? The key to successfully introducing your pup to new rooms of your house is to take it one step at a time, very slowly and in a very controlled manner. At first, don't allow access to all rooms of the house. Gradually expand your pup's living quarters, one room at a time, and only when you are there to supervise. When you first allow a pup into a new room he won't realize that it is part of the "den, " and therefore won't realize he needs to keep

How you clean up accidents in the house is crucial.

it clean. That's where your careful planning and supervision comes in. Take him outside to potty before you go to the new area. Once there, keep part of your attention on him, whether you're reading a magazine or watching TV. Pet him, talk to him, and if he falls asleep by your side, all the better. Feed him his dinner, play with him and do some training in his new room so that as time goes on, he will begin to think of it as part of his home and do his best to keep it clean.

PROBLEMS? If at any point you find your pup regressing and making mistakes—even mistakes you thought he was past making—don't despair. This is common and nothing to worry about; all learning curves go up and down a bit. Although it may be a bit frustrating for you, try to relax and just help your pup get it right by backing up in your training.

> *Don't worry about occasional back sliding – all learning curves go up and down a bit.*

Go back to taking him out more, watching him more closely, and confining him more judiciously when you can't keep your attention on him. Basically, go back to the beginning and start teaching him again. It won't take nearly as long the second (or third) time around. Try looking at how fast you were progressing; perhaps it was too fast for him to get a thorough understanding of what he needed to learn. Have faith! It will come with time.

LAST WORD OF ADVICE If your pup seems to be urinating more often than normal or having a lot of trouble with housetraining, see your veterinarian to rule out health problems. Dogs can get urinary tract infections just like people, which makes it hard for them to control their bladders. There can also be other medical reasons for urinary incontinence, so check out his health if you have any doubts about it at all.

SUMMARY

• Puppies need enjoyable exposure to a variety of people, other dogs and different environments to develop into stable, adaptable adults.

• Positive reinforcement (which is something your puppy loves, not something that makes you happy!) is the most effective way to influence a dog's behavior. Using treats to teach a new behavior isn't "bribing," it's creating good habits that will last a lifetime.

• Don't expect your dog to pay attention to you just because you want her to! Teach her it's to her advantage to pay attention to you by taking her out of the house and giving her a treat when she looks at you.

• Use the "Lure/Reward" method to teach your pup to sit and lie down on cue, first eliciting the action you want by "luring" and then immediately rewarding her with a treat.

• Successful housetraining requires you to manage your puppy at all times: she should be either outside with you (and getting a treat for going potty in the right area), under careful supervision in the house, or in a crate or small sleeping area. It's labor intensive at the beginning, but doing it correctly will save you endless problems in the long run.

2
NEXT STEPS

★ SPECIAL TOPIC

PLAY BITING

A mouth with paws: That's a good description of a lot of our puppies when they first come to us. Even the best of dogs have to learn to be polite with their mouths, just as children have to learn not to slap with their hands. Pups come to us having weeks or months of play that included biting on their littermates, so from their perspective, why shouldn't they chomp on our fingers? Your job now, while your dog is still young and has relatively weak jaws[1], is to teach your puppy two things simultaneously: 1) *bite inhibition*, meaning how to modulate the power of his jaws to avoid hurting a person or another dog and 2) that play biting is best done on toys and other dogs, not on people.

WHY CAN'T I LET MY DOG BITE ME? At the risk of sounding like the play police, we strongly advise against playing with your pup in ways that encourage him to mouth or bite you. It will only confuse your pup about the appropriate use of his teeth. If you allow him to bite you, even playfully, you are teaching him that human hands are for play biting. You yourself might not mind that, but it will confuse him when he gets in trouble for biting grandma or the little toddler down the street. He won't realize it's not okay to do the same thing to them.

---

1 Those of you with bloody hands may well roll your eyes at the phrase "weak jaws," but compared to what your dog can do as an adult, those jaws really are weak, honest. It's just that those tiny teeth are SO sharp!

So don't confuse him and get him into trouble. Don't roughhouse with your pup, and don't let others do so either. We talk about this in detail in Chapter 4, but it's important enough to merit a comment here.

TEACHING BITE INHIBITION

Begin your training by teaching bite inhibition, while your pup is young and mouthy and is obsessed with wrapping his mouth around your hands (legs, ankles, arms, face, hair…). You have a head start in a way, because your pup has probably learned a bit about bite inhibition already. As pups play with each other, one pup or another is bound to bite a littermate too hard. The recipient will let out a sharp yelp in response to the discomfort. The game ends suddenly and all play stops. With repetition puppies eventually learn to play in a gentler fashion with one another so that they don't lose their playmates. However, even little puppies have tougher skin than we do—all that fur is a great insulator, and our lack of it makes our skin especially sensitive. That means we need to teach our pups that even the slightest pressure ends the game.

WHY BOTHER? Even though you are wise to discourage your dog from using you as a toy at all, it is still worthwhile to teach him to modulate his jaw power around people. Adult dogs who never learned finesse with their mouths as youngsters might be more likely to cause serious injury, either while playing or intentionally biting. No one wants to think of their little fuzz ball as a potential biter, but if your dog can open and shut his mouth, he can bite. Even the sweetest dog can strike out if injured or frightened. It could either be a warning snap, or a serious injury to the child next door. That's why it is worthwhile to teach bite inhibition now, as a preventative measure, just as you use vaccinations to prevent serious health problems.

HERE'S HOW To teach your dog to be careful with his mouth, first try yelping like another puppy whenever you feel your pup's mouth putting pressure on any part of your body. We use the word "AWRP!" (sounding something like a startled seal), but you can say OUCH! or EEPS! or whatever comes out of your mouth naturally. *How* you say it is more important than *what* you say—the sound should be sudden, abrupt, and relatively loud. It should start and stop almost instantly, going from silence to full volume in a microsecond. Avoid long, drawn out "No-o-o-o-o-o-o-'s." That kind of sound will have little or no effect. The point is to startle your pup just as he bites down. (It's a good idea to practice this when your pup is not around, so you'll be good at it when you need it. Try it, honest, it'll help!) Begin by yelping only on the hardest bites, ignoring the softer bites. As you progress, yelp at gradually softer and softer pressure from your pup until he eventually mouths you with no pressure at all.

REPLACE YOUR HAND WITH A TOY After you yelp, (and we mean *immediately* afterward), offer your pup an appropriate toy. Move it around about a foot in front of his face (if the toy is too close it often discourages play) and encourage him to bite onto it. This won't work unless you present the toy instantly after you yelp, because playful puppies just HAVE to put something in their mouths. If you don't give them something appropriate, they'll go right back to biting on you. That means you need to have a toy ready at all times—carry one around in your pocket and each time you use one, be sure to pick up another so that you always have one at the ready. After a day or two this will become second nature (and encourage pants with large pockets).

> *Have a toy ready at all times—carry one around in your pocket & encourage your pup to bite on it instead of you.*

Yelping and redirecting can teach your pup two things: 1) humans are absurdly sensitive, so he needs to modulate the power of his jaws around them and 2) it's much more fun to play with a dog toy than someone's hand or ankle.

NOT WORKING? Some puppies haven't read the chapter on canine development, and don't respond to a yelp or an "Ouch!" as we'd hope. A small percentage of pups become more excited if you yelp. Give it a try, but if your pup becomes more excited, then switch to the method outlined below. In all training, guard against doing the same thing over and over again if it's not working. A good method should result in at least some improvement within three to five repetitions.

Yelping doesn't seem to work as well if young children do it. If you have young children, you will need to make the noise for them. Children's voices are often too high and too weak to impress the message on a puppy, and sometimes yelping from little ones seems to excite the puppy rather than inhibit him. However, it often works well for a nearby adult to watch the child and dog (which should always be the case anyway) and yelp "OUCH" just as the puppy's mouth is closing around the child's skin (or hair, or clothes, etc.). The adult or child should then immediately redirect the puppy onto an appropriate toy. Eventually, when the puppy is excited around a child he will look for the nearest toy to mouth on, instead of the child.

ANOTHER METHOD Another method to try, especially if your pup is being very persistent or if children are involved, is to dramatically jump up and leave the room in a big huff when he bites too hard. Don't talk, don't explain, just march out quickly, without looking back, and shut the door behind you. If your timing is good, your pup will associate his behavior with losing his playmate. Pups do the equivalent of this with one another, and in some cases it can be very effective. If your pup goes after your ankles as you leave the room, then simply stop moving and stand still. If he is still biting when you ignore him, try spraying your pant legs and shoestrings with something like Bitter Apple® to make the nipping taste bad. After giving him a 'cold shoulder' for several seconds, try re-engaging, but lead in with a toy so you can direct his biting to an appropriate object. If you need to do this more than 4-5 times within a few minutes of play, then it might not a good time to be interacting with your pup. Perhaps he needs to burn off a little energy first by doing a few laps around the living room or yard before you try to interact closely with him. Or, perhaps he is hungry, thirsty, needs to potty, or is overly tired and needs a nap.

HAVE PATIENCE! Be prepared for your pup to try to play with you as a toy again and again. Puppies will tend to forget themselves during the next play session and come back and bite again. Some will be very persistent about it, others will switch to a different mode more quickly. They are all individuals, but eventually they will all learn to modulate their own behavior. It doesn't mean your puppy is mean or vicious if it takes him more time and many repetitions to stop nipping you, it just means you'll need to be persistent until he gets the idea. However, if play biting isn't decreasing, or hasn't been eliminated from your dog's play repertoire by the time he is six months old, you'd be wise to contact a trainer or behaviorist for some customized coaching.

 NEW EXERCISES

COMING WHEN CALLED

WELL WORTH THE EFFORT One of the most valuable things you can teach your dog is to come when called. Ironically, the more control you have over your dog, the more freedom you can give him, so the time you spend on this exercise is more than worth the effort. If your dog comes running on cue, you can call him in from the backyard when you're late for work, call him away from a potential fight at the dog park, and call him to you after he saw a deer in the woods. That means you can take him on walks in the woods, let him play at the dog park with his buddies and lounge in a fenced backyard when he feels like it. Thus, teaching a dog to come when called is as important to his happiness as it is to yours.

FIRST, TRAIN YOURSELF! Decide what signal you're going to use to call your dog, and use it consistently. This may sound easy, but most of us are not very good at it.[2] We say "Buster, Come!," followed by "Come Here, Buster" and my personal favorite "BUSTER!!!!" (Buster, what?) Teach yourself and your family to use one word or phrase, and say it the same way every time. The best cues are short, punchy kinds of sounds like "Drift! Come!" or "Pup! Pup! Pup!" Hand claps work especially well: In Patricia's research on acoustics and canine responses, it was found that hand claps were the most successful of ten different sounds (like claps, words and whistles) to get puppies to run to the sound source.

Your body can talk to your dog too. How you position your body has a big effect on your dog's behavior. If you stand squarely facing your

---

2 Understatement alert: Most of us are actually terrible at being consistent when we talk to our dogs, but the more consistent you are, the more consistent your dog will be.

dog or move toward him, your pup is more likely to stay away. Your voice may be saying "come," but to your dog, your body is saying "I'm warning you, don't come any closer!" Dogs like to chase, so when you call your dog to come, turn your body sideways, and move *away* from your dog as you call. Your movement away will draw your dog toward you, rather than blocking him from moving forward. You'll have to concentrate on this at first; it's not natural to turn your body and move away from your dog as you call him to come.

NOW, WORK ON YOUR DOG! Now that you've starting training yourself (!), start training your pup. Start in an area with few distractions—always set your puppy up to win when you are introducing a new exercise. From no more than ten feet away, call out your dog's new cue, turn your body sideways, and then start clapping and running away from your dog. *As soon as he moves* even a few inches in your direction, sing out "Good Dog!" and keep going. When he catches up to you, have a party! Praise him to the skies and give him extra tasty treats. If he likes it, give him some great rubs on his chest or rump.

Keep in mind that the hardest part of a "recall" (trainer talk for "coming when called") is when your dog has to turn his attention away from what he's doing and onto you. (Ever said "Just a minute" without turning your head when someone said your name?). That's why you should sing out "Good boy!" the instant he starts moving toward you, or turns his head in your direction. He needs reinforcing long before he arrives at your feet. Here's where you get to reap the rewards of linking praise with a food treat. Because he's learned that praise leads to food, he'll be reinforced when he needs to be, right after he begins doing what you want him to do. When he arrives, praise him some more and pop a tasty treat in his mouth.[3] Now he's been reinforced three times: once with your praise for shifting his attention onto you, again as he gets to chase you while you run in another direction, and a third time with praise and food for arriving at your feet.

---

3 This isn't the time to ask for a sit, because then he'll think the treat is for sitting, not coming when called.

BE CAREFUL HOW YOU REINFORCE A word to the wise: dogs aren't as fond of receiving head pats as we are of giving them. In every puppy class you can watch owners pat-pat-patting the top of their recently recalled dogs' heads, believing that they are reinforcing their dogs for coming. However, if you watch for it, you can see the dogs ducking down and turning their heads away as if they didn't like it. Remember, you're trying to create an association between feeling good and coming when called, so be sure that what you're doing is truly making your dog happy. He'll tell you if you watch closely—does he stay with you, wagging from the shoulders back (good)? Or does he turn his head away from you and try to leave (time for another plan!).

WHEN AND WHERE Repeat this game several times a day in short sessions, conditioning your dog to link the cue "come" with running toward you and feeling good about it. Be sure to scatter these sessions throughout the day, playing the game in different areas of your home. You'll want to call him to come to you at least 20 or 30 times a day during early training. No kidding! Puppies come hard wired to attend to you until they hit adolescence (around 4 to 5 months of age), so take advantage of this early developmental period now, and teach yours to come on cue when it is easiest and most effective.

However, be thoughtful about when you call your dog to come. At this stage, avoid calling your dog to come if he's intensely focused on something else. Your goal is to create a foundation of coming *every* time he's called, so don't set your dog up to fail (and to learn to ignore you when he feels like it). If you eventually want a dog to come away from a vigorous play session with other puppies, then you need to start with him coming *every* time he's called and being really glad that he did. This sounds simple, but it turns out to be one of the greatest challenges for novice dog owners. It's tempting to call a dog to come without thinking through the difficulty of the exercise, thereby setting him up to fail. Always consider the level of competing distractions before you call your dog to come when he's still in training. We find it useful to think of come training like levels of mathematical ability.

Be sure that your dog loves the petting you provide as reinforcement—otherwise, it won't work.

For your dog, coming to you when there's nothing else going on, and you're holding a piece of chicken, is as easy as adding two and two. Coming away from the fresh scent of deer tracks in the back yard is as challenging as doing calculus! Would you expect a five-year old child to be able to do advanced math? How about expecting a student to skip from simple addition to complicated mathematical formulas without learning algebra? You'd never expect that of your child (we hope), so don't expect it of your dog.

If you're pretty sure your dog is too distracted to respond in any particular situation, simply *go to him* with a treat in hand, show him the treat and lure him to where you want him to go. If that's not enough, gently snap on his leash and ease him along to where you need to go. Be sure to avoid calling your pup for something he's not going to enjoy, like getting a nail trim or going into his crate if he's still full of energy. In that case, simply go to him and snap on his leash, keeping a friendly and upbeat attitude, being sure to avoid linking the word "come" with something he doesn't like.

There's nothing like watching your dog joyfully run toward you when you call, so keep that image in mind and play the come game whenever you have an extra minute or two. This is the time to work on getting a great recall for years to come, so don't let the opportunity slip by!

TEACHING STAND

Yep, your dog knows how to stand on all four paws without any help from you, but it's handy to teach a cue that means "stand up and stay still for a moment." You can use it to have her stand still while you wipe muddy paws, stand up for the veterinarian or make it easier for you to groom her. Once your puppy learns Stand, try asking for several cues in a row, such as "Sit-Down-Stand-Sit." You'll experience the importance of timing and fast reactions, because once you get your pup standing up, you're only going to have a split second to keep her attention on the next cue . . . or off she'll go!

GETTING STARTED Start by putting a treat in your hand, and asking your pup to sit. Put the food about an inch away from her nose, but this time move it slowly forward, away from her face. Keep the movement parallel to the floor. Don't move your hand up or down, keep it level with her nose, and move it just fast enough to get her attention, but slowly enough to keep her nose "connected" with the scent of the treat. If she wants to follow the treat, she'll have to get up to do so. The microsecond she is up on all fours, stop your forward hand motion, praise her and pop the treat into her mouth.

Once you know she'll stand up readily when you move your hand outward from her nose, introduce the word cue by saying "Stand" a good second before you make a move. Link the word (first) with the movement (second) together several times, but once you've done several successful repetitions, try just saying the word but not moving. This will probably take longer than it does with sit training—dogs seem to learn to sit to a verbal cue fastest, but lying down and standing up in response to nothing but a spoken word takes a bit longer. Use the visual cue to help her get it right for as long as she needs, but work to decouple the sound and the movement into two different cues as soon as you can.

 PRACTICE MAKES PERFECT

SIT AND DOWN REVISITED

The luring motion that you have been making with your hand to elicit the sit and down position is already the beginning of a visual cue. It's a wonderful thing to have a dog trained to sit and lie down to both a visual and a word cue. However, we often use these signals simultaneously, so our dogs don't learn them as separate cues. Both types of cues have their benefits: Visual cues are easier for dogs to learn—their social communication is primarily through posture and expression, so they are quick to pick up on our movements. Visual cues can be used when your dog is far away, in noisy situations or when you're talking on the

It's a wonderful thing to have a dog trained to sit and lie down to both a visual and a word cue.

phone and need your dog to sit instead of chasing the cat. On the other hand, words, or acoustic cues, are our primary way of communicating, which is why we expect our dogs to listen to us. In addition, we need our dogs to respond to us even when they aren't looking at us. Thus, it's extremely useful to teach your dog both visual and verbal cues as separate signals, and this is how you do it:

SIT TO A VISUAL CUE This week, your primary job with sit and down training is to focus on creating clear and consistent cues for your dog. First, concentrate on the movement of your hand when you ask your pup to sit. Don't use a word right now; keep things clear by using only one cue at a time. Signal your pup to sit two times in a row by using the treat as a lure, as you did in the beginning. The third time, keep the treat in your hand, put it close to your dog's nose, but then sweep your hand upward toward your chest. You'll have to finesse this. Some dogs will sit instantly when you move the treat up rather than back over their heads, while others will need you to make a hybrid movement that splits the difference. In the latter case, move your hand only slightly upward at first to raise your dog's chin, then gradually begin sweeping your hand further up and toward your chest.

Your goal is to teach your dog to sit when you move your hand upward (notice this still causes her to raise her chin, thus encouraging her to sit back on her haunches). Gradually work toward less and less luring, and toward using a cue in which you stand up straight and sweep your hand upward toward your face as you look at your pup. Most pups pick up on this extremely fast. Don't worry if your pup regresses one day after doing brilliantly the day before; just take a step back and create a success, then try again to lure less and use the cue more. Once your cue is effective, try signaling your pup without having a treat in your hand. When she sits, surprise her with a treat from the other hand. Voilá! You have a dog who sits to a hand signal!

SIT TO THE WORD "SIT" We all want our dogs to sit when we say the word, but most people are surprised to learn that most dogs primarily attend to our movements. Of course, all dogs can eventually learn to do hundreds of things to your voice alone, but it helps to consciously separate sound and movement while training. Toward that end, in the early stages of training, pay attention to what you are doing when you ask your dog to sit. Focus on saying "sit" *before* you move your hand to lure him into position.

Once your dog is sitting readily to a visual cue (which could be in just a few sessions), start a new session as usual by saying "sit" before you move your hand. Try that three times in a row, but the fourth time say "sit" without moving your hand at all. After saying "sit," force yourself to wait 2 seconds to give your pup a chance to sit just to your voice. Often a pup will stare at you, waiting for a movement from you, and then the light will dawn and she'll sit down, albeit a bit tentatively. If she does, GOOD GIRL! Praise effusively and give her a couple of extra great treats.

As the week progresses, work on using clear and consistent cues, remembering that if you always say "sit" and move your hand at the same time, your dog will be less likely to respond to the word alone. This is a perfect time to acknowledge, as all good trainers do, that much of "dog training" is "people training!" None of us are inherently good at being consistent and uniform in our speech or movements, but if we're not, how are our dogs supposed to understand us? Practice being consistent yourself while you're training your dog . . . it'll pay off for both of you, we promise.

VARY THE REINFORCEMENTS

Food is a convenient and effective way to teach something new to a dog, but it's also valuable to get in the habit of varying the reinforcements you use to reward her. This is a perfect time to teach her that doing what you ask is both fun and to her advantage. If you intersperse food with other reinforcements she'll generalize from "If I sit when asked I'll get a treat" to "If I sit when asked I'll feel good." For most dogs, it works best to use food when you are teaching something new or when your pup is likely to be distracted (asking for a sit in the backyard instead of the kitchen for example), but start interspersing other reinforcements once you've gotten a behavior established. Every dog is different, so it's up to you to learn what your pup likes best, and what you can use most effectively as reinforcement.

For example, once your pup is getting good at sit, surprise her as she walks with you from one room to the next by saying "sit" out of the blue. Praise her and then dash away, letting her chase you as a game. Ask for sit and down and then giggle and rub her belly. Call "come," run away, pick up a favorite toy and throw it for her when she arrives at your feet. The more you generalize the reinforcements, the more likely she'll be to respond anytime and anywhere.

 **★ SPECIAL TOPIC**

CRATE TRAINING

Crates can be your pup's best friend, but you need to teach a puppy to be comfortable in one. In spite of what some say, dogs aren't "den animals." The only time they use a den is just before giving birth, and for a few weeks after the pups are born. Once the puppies are about two months old, the den is abandoned and the dogs sleep above ground.

However, it's great to have a way to keep puppies out of trouble, since none of us can watch them every second of the day. In addition, crates give your dog a secure sleeping place, along with giving you the ability to prevent the development of bad habits. Remember that prevention is a powerful training tool, so it only makes sense to confine your pup in some way when you aren't with her.

USE CRATE REST WHEN:
• You are too busy to watch your pup.

• You are leaving the house for awhile.

• Your puppy is being wild and crazy and needs a little "time out" (or you do!).

• When you are sleeping.

Commercial crates give you a lot of options now, from plastic airline-type crates, to wire and cloth ones. Cloth crates might be a bit too tempting for busy puppy mouths, but can work well for lots of older dogs. Wire crates are often best if you cover the top and sides so that your pup feels cozy and secure, but give you the option of providing ventilation if it's warm. However, every situation is different, so choose what works best for you. You can also keep your dog in a small puppy-proofed room, such as a vinyl-floored laundry room or a kitchen. Use puppy gates and "Ex-pens" (flexible fences that you can put up anywhere) to keep your pup secure in an area without doors.

Crates can be your other best friend, but you need to teach a pup to be comfortable in one.

LOCATION LOCATION LOCATION If you are using a crate, put it in a room that you use often. You want your pup to feel like he is an area that feels and smells like "home." Don't exile your pup to some lonely spot in the house. If you need your dog to be in a rarely used room, you can make it comfy by spending time in the room with him. You want the room to feel comfy and cozy, not like an unfamiliar warehouse. Settle into the designated area with your pup and a paperback, and hang out for an hour or so, several times a week. Whatever room you use, put the crate off to one side, or in a corner, so it is out of the way of traffic. Don't put it smack in the middle of a traffic zone in which your dog will constantly be stimulated and disturbed. In addition, don't put it by a window to "entertain" your pup. You'll just end up over stimulating and frustrating him. We advise keeping the crate in the bedroom at night, so your puppy is sleeping with you, but is unable to potty on the carpet while you snore into your pillow.

TEACHING YOUR PUP TO ENJOY THE CRATE It is a good idea to condition your pup to like being in his crate, even if you've already started using it. You can't lose by taking it slowly and teaching your dog to feel good when he enters and stays in his crate (even if it seems like you are going backward in your training!). Begin with your pup near the crate, off leash, with the crate door open. Show him that you have a really wonderful treat by moving it to within an inch of his nose. Next, move the treat slowly toward the crate door, "luring" him toward the crate with the food.

Once your pup is close to the door of the crate, toss the treat just inside the crate. Hopefully he will reach his head into the crate opening to get the treat. It doesn't matter that he doesn't go all the way in at first, you can build up to that by throwing the treat farther into his crate each time you practice this. (If the food you're using doesn't tempt him, try something better, like real meat). Be sure not to force any part of this. You want him to enter voluntarily and be glad that he did.

Let him come out of the crate right away, don't try to close the door yet. Toss treats in again, four or five times in a row, gradually throwing them so that he has to go all the way into the crate. Each time, let him turn around and come out. Your job right now is to teach him that entering the crate is really fun! Once he goes inside willingly, put it on cue by saying "crate up" or "go to bed" a second before he enters the kennel to get the treat.

If he is too afraid to go in at all, set the treat on the floor just *outside* the kennel door and let him take his time. Get him comfortable eating it outside, but near the crate, before trying to put the food just inside the door. Make sure he's comfortable at each stage before moving the food farther and farther into the crate. Repeat this game 4-6 times each session. Keep it fun, don't force or drag him into the crate, which could easily make him more afraid of it.

Repeat this game several times until he dashes into the crate enthusiastically. That could take one session or several, depending on your dog. Once he enters cheerfully, shut the door for *just a second* while he's inside eating his treats. Repeat this four to five times, changing the game a little to get him used to the door swinging shut. Open the door immediately at first, and then work up to keeping it shut for several seconds. As you increase the time in the crate, toss in a handful of treats or put a hollow toy (stuffed with food) in the crate with him. Feeding him his meals in the kennel also helps him learn to be comfortable when confined.

You can also lure him into the crate when he's sleepy. Young puppies especially have "off/on" switches, and once they are tired, they sleep as if drugged. You'll be able to predict when your pup is getting tired, and take advantage of his natural cycles to crate him up before he nods off.

LET ME OUT! At some point your dog is bound to try barking or whining to get out of the crate. This is natural, it's his way of trying to let you know that he wants out or desires your company. It is important however that you *do not* inadvertently reinforce the barking or whining by letting him out (or telling him "it's okay") *while* he's making a fuss. Instead, ignore him until he quiets down on his own. If they're not reinforced for making a fuss, most pups will learn to settle down and be quiet when left in their crate or sleeping room.

If he starts barking relentlessly, and you're beginning to pull your hair out by the roots, do whatever you need to do to cope (ear plugs? wine?) but don't shout at him to "BE QUIET!" If you do, you are basically barking back, and as anyone with multiple dogs knows, barking is contagious! Even if your dog understands that you are irritated, you've still given him attention, and that, after all, is what he wanted. If you need to get him out of the kennel when he's crying or barking, distract him with a noise (click of the tongue, tap on the wall, anything that gets his attention) to get him quiet for a moment. The *instant* that he is quiet you can let him out of the kennel.

The one exception is if your pup is trying to tell you that he has to potty. If you think this might be the case, take him outside quietly, give him his "go potty" cue, treat and praise when he does and then put him right back in the crate.

PREVENT TROUBLE WHEN YOU CAN Try to put him in the crate when he's tuckered out whenever you can. When you do, give him something safe to chew on and be sure he's eliminated outside before he goes into his crate. He will most likely sleep if all his needs are tended to before you put him in the crate. And don't leave him there for hour after hour. Limit the time he's left alone to just a few hours at a time, especially when he is very young. Arrange for someone to let your puppy out every four hours or so if you have to be gone all day. Crates can be overused. Leaving a three-month old puppy in a crate for nine hours is setting him up for failure and frustration. But if used judiciously, crates can be one of your best allies in teaching your pup how to be calm and quiet in the house.

SUMMARY

• Discourage your puppy from using you as a toy: teach bite inhibition by yelping when she bites you in play, and immediately redirect her to an appropriate toy. Have toys handy at all times, including carrying them in your pocket so that you can engage your pup in appropriate play any time, any where.

• Now is the time to start conditioning your pup to come when called. Decide on one cue and use it consistently; call your puppy to come and run away from her, clapping and praising as she moves toward you. Give her a treat as soon as she catches up, without asking her to sit first.

• Begin to use your visual and acoustic sit cues separately. Use both together, as usual, three times in a row, and then ask your pup to sit to one or the other. Pay attention to your own behavior here, using this week to train yourself to notice exactly what you are doing when you are asking your dog to sit or lie down.

• Teach your pup to stand on cue by luring her into a stand from a sit.

• Once a response has become reliable (say asking your puppy to sit in a quiet room), begin varying the kinds of reinforcements you offer. Continue to make your pup glad she did what you asked, but mix it up with treats, play, belly rubs and chase games.

• Condition your dog to relax in a crate by going step-by-step. Throw treats inside the crate and let your pup enter to eat them, and immediately come back out again. Once she'll enter readily, give her a hollow toy stuffed with food and leave her in the crate for gradually increasing amounts of time. Don't expect young puppies to control their bladders in a crate all day long—arrange for someone to let your pup out every 4 hours or so if you are gone during the day.

3
PLEASE STOP DOING THAT!
(DO THIS, INSTEAD!)

★ SPECIAL TOPICS

HOW TO STOP UNWANTED BEHAVIOR

Inevitably, at some point your pup will do something that is so much fun that she doesn't want stop. Regrettably, that might be chewing on your wallet or your ankle. Fun for her, but not so much for you. The fact is, all puppies are engaged in learning about their environment, and they do that by relentlessly exploring it. Thus, inevitably, they are bound to do things and get into things that they shouldn't.[4] Someone once said that if you can't bear to lose a pair of good shoes then you probably shouldn't get a puppy. Your puppy is to some extent predictable—the question is, what about your behavior? How are you going to handle it when your pup does something you don't want her to do? Your response can prevent problems and strengthen the bond between you and your dog, or create serious trouble that results in a distrustful, adversarial relationship. Here are illustrative examples of both choices:

A DOG NAMED TASHA Tasha is a normal 11 week-old puppy—active, inquisitive, and curious. She explores and investigates her world with her teeth, just as all puppies do. One day Tasha notices a small plastic object sitting on a low table in the family room. Everyone in the family

4 If you've had your new dog for longer than five minutes, you already knew that.

handles this item often and it smells like Mom, Dad and the kids. Since this "toy" (the remote control) is right at nose level and is in easy reach, Tasha grabs it off the table. After a few minutes of satisfying chewing, Mom enters the room, spots Tasha chewing on the remote and yells "NO BAD DOG!" at the top of her lungs. She grabs Tasha by the collar and shakes her, continuing to scold her with a harsh tone. Mom yanks the "toy" out of Tasha's mouth and abruptly shoves her in her crate, swatting Tasha's rump just before closing the door. Tasha is confused, frightened, and not at all sure what just transpired. Mom isn't usually like that, and it was kind of scary.

A few days later, Tasha finds the remote control on the floor where one of the kids left it. The little "toy" even smells like the butter Joey had on his fingers from eating popcorn. Tasha can't resist! She lies down and begins licking, then chewing on the crunchy little plastic thing. After awhile Tasha gets distracted and runs off to see what smells good in the kitchen.

Later, Dad notices the chewed up (and now ruined) remote control. That's the last straw after a tough day, and in anger he yells at Tasha to "come here right now!" He grabs Tasha by the scruff of the neck and pushes her face into the ruined remote, saying "NO NO NO" in a loud voice. Finally Dad grabs Tasha and shoves her in her crate.

What did Tasha learn here? Well, let's look at what happened from her perspective: She learned that chewing on the remote is super fun unless a human sees her doing it. Tasha learned to head the other way when she hears "come," because coming when called resulted in being scared and confused. She learned that human hands can hurt her and should be avoided. She may learn to growl at people to guard her "treasures," since people only reach for them to steal them away. She may never quite trust Mom or Dad (and possibly other humans) since they seem unpredictable and dangerous at times. Finally, Tasha learned that her crate is not necessarily a good place after all.

Let's look at another example that begins with the same set of circumstances, but has a very different outcome.

THE STORY OF PUZZLE   Like Tasha, Puzzle is a normal 11-week-old pup.   However, Puzzle's family "puppy-proofed" the house and provided Puzzle with lots of exciting toys.   Puzzle doesn't get lonely or bored in the family room, because a family member is always with Puzzle whenever she is in that room. They provide lots of appropriate chewy things for Puzzle to bite on, knowing that puppies pretty much have to chew on something.

Also like Tasha, Puzzle noticed the remote control sitting on the coffee table, with its easy access, good smells, and fun little buttons all over it. But Puzzle was never left in this room alone, and Mom saw the focus of Puzzle's interest.   Mom, being wise to the ways of puppies, picked it up and put it out of Puzzle's reach.   Then she redirected Puzzle to a dog toy, by wiggling it around and throwing just a few feet away from Puzzle.   Puzzle couldn't resist chasing it and immediately forgot the remote control.

A few days later when the remote control was on the floor covered with the smell of popcorn and butter (oh those kids!), Puzzle found it and was ready to settle in for a good chew. Dad looked up and saw what Puzzle was doing and responded by clapping his hands together to get her attention, and then called her to come in a friendly, happy voice. Puzzle looked at the remote—oh so tempting!, but Dad clapped again and bounced a ball that he had handy in his pocket. As Puzzle looked at him, making up her mind, he said "Good Girl!" and ran the other way to entice her to chase him. Puzzle couldn't resist the potential of treats and a good game of tag, and dashed off after him, leaving the remote to be picked up later when Puzzle was busy elsewhere.

Over the following weeks Mom and Dad made sure that the remote control was either picked up out of Puzzle's reach at all times, or that Puzzle was stopped and redirected whenever she tried to help herself to it.

What did Puzzle learn?   First of all, she learned that Mom and Dad are the source of fun, and that they can be trusted and loved. She was developing the good habit of chewing only on dog toys and avoiding the bad habit of chewing on remotes or other inappropriate objects. Puzzle is on her way to establishing good habits that will serve her and her family well. She is getting clear, instructive feedback from her environment and helpful guidance from her owners, rather than learning to fear and mistrust them. She will figure out the "rules" to living in her family's house quickly. She will make plenty of mistakes, as all youngsters do, but her family is managing her and her environment to facilitate good behavior and inhibit problems.

You might think that this last story is reminiscent of some 1950's family sit com, in which everyone is well-mannered and mom wears high heels while baking cookies in the kitchen, but it's not that hard to pull off—at least, *most* of the time. All of us makes mistakes, and raising puppies always includes some training glitches, but once you get in the habit of raising a puppy the right way, it gets easier and easier. Here are the keys to helping your pup learn what is and isn't appropriate in your home:

BE CONSISTENT Decide what your family's rules will be, and enlist the whole family to work together as a team to consistently maintain those rules. If Dad lets Ginger play bite, Ginger won't understand she's not supposed to do the same with Grandma or little Susie. If Grandma lets Ginger cuddle next to her on the couch any time she wants, Ginger won't understand if Mom gets angry at her for jumping up in Mom's lap when she sits down. Have clearly defined family rules so that you don't confuse your puppy. Granted, getting everyone in a family to follow those rules consistently is a challenge, but do your best. The more consistent the environment, the better the puppy's behavior.

PREVENTION PREVENTION PREVENTION It is your responsibility to prevent your puppy from learning bad habits, pure and simple. This sounds easy enough, but in practice it takes a thoughtful appraisal of the house, an ability to always have part of your attention focused on your pup, and the acknowledgment that we all mess up from time

> *Have clearly defined family rules so that you don't confuse your puppy.*

to time. If you haven't already, walk around your house and pick up anything that might tempt your dog, or that might harm her if she chews on it (be especially careful with electric cords). Puppy-proof your home and supervise your puppy until she learns the rules. Eventually she will learn how to be good without supervision, but that will take many months of guidance and training. You wouldn't leave a toddler alone in a room unsupervised, would you? Well, your pup has just as much to learn about how to be "good" as a human child does, so don't set your puppy up to fail. Prevent mishaps before they happen.

REDIRECT Always be ready to interrupt your pup from doing something inappropriate and to redirect her toward something that is appropriate. Have a toy in your pocket to redirect her from the muddy shoes by the door (oh yum!) to a designated dog toy. Lure her away from chewing on the fern in the living room by asking her to sit, down and stand several times in a row, and then toss her a hollow dog toy stuffed with treats while you move the fern out of reach or spray it with a commercial product that deters chewing. Over and over (and truly, that's exactly what it feels like!) direct her to an option other than the behavior that could get her into trouble. She will eventually learn that she has other options, and she will begin to make better choices.

> *Always be ready to interrupt your pup from doing something inappropriate and to redirect her to something that is.*

TEACH "WHOOPS!" It's helpful to be able to communicate to a dog that something she is doing is wrong, without scaring or hurting her. Toward that end, consider teaching your pup a cue that simply means "Please stop doing that, it's not allowed here, and turn your attention to me." You can use any word you want. A lot of people say "No!" and there's nothing wrong with that IF you can continue to use it as a cue and not a punishment. That's a big "if!" It seems seductive to use the word "no" in a loud, gruff voice, and many of us automatically shout out an angry "NO" when a pup does something we don't like. But then, when the first "No" is ignored, it escalates into getting louder and louder, and angrier and angrier. If the pup has no idea what the sound means, all you are communicating is that you are aroused and potentially aggressive. You are not telling the pup what she is doing wrong, nor telling her what she *should* be doing.

Use whatever cue you like best, "Whoops," or "No" or "Uh Uh," but only use it after you've taught your pup what it means. You can do this easily by setting up a situation in which she'll be tempted to do something inappropriate, but over which you have control. For example, get some tasty treats in your non-dominant hand, and put down something that your pup should never chew on. Place it so that you can easily step between it and your puppy. As your pup goes to sniff it, say "Whoops" and move forward, blocking your pup's path. As she looks up at you, click or praise and treat. Repeat that two or three times with the same object, until she automatically looks up at you when you place the object on the ground. When she does that, eureka! Give her several treats in a row, and make a big fuss.

A bit later, try it again with something else, always using things she's not supposed to bother, and always being ready to reinforce her the instant she takes her attention off of the object. Gradually work your way up to expecting her to respond to your "Whoops" when she is more and more distracted, but be aware it can take many months for a pup to have enough emotional control to turn away from a dropped pork chop!

HELP! SHE HAS MY $300 GLASSES! Sometimes you have to respond instantly to something that could become a financial or safety-related crisis. In that case, consider using what's called a "remote correction," which is a way of interrupting your pup without actually being right beside her. It can consist of anything that startles the puppy from whatever she was doing—a slap against the wall (just to make a noise) or a beanbag tossed on the floor near the pup. We've used a magazine, a paperback book, and in the case of a pup about to gobble up spilled medicine on the other side of the room (which could have killed her), a shoe jerked off of a foot in desperation. The point is to toss an object *near* her to *startle* her, (not to hit her with anything!) Be sure to use only enough drama to get your pup's attention; you don't want to traumatize her, just get her attention off what she was doing. This method should only be used in times of crisis. Most of the time you should be working on teaching her the "Whoops" cue, but stuff happens, and it's better to be ready for it rather than blind-sided.

AVOID PHYSICAL CORRECTIONS Physical corrections should not be a routine part of your pup's education. If you find that is happening, please seek out a good trainer and/or behaviorist to help you get your relationship with your dog back on track. Frequent physical corrections indicate a lack of communication and understanding between you and your canine pal.

• Here are a few last words about corrections, given that it's a rare family that can raise a puppy without using them on occasion:

• First of all, a correction should not involve anger. Corrections are to teach and educate your pup. You probably don't learn much when someone is angrily screaming in your face or hitting you, and your pup won't either. Does that mean you'll never find yourself a tad irritated by your pup? Ha! If you find yourself losing your temper, take a deep breath, and in the sweetest voice imaginable, say: "You are one ugly puppy." Take advantage of the fact that dogs don't come speaking English, and get rid of your frustration through language, just keep saying it like it's sweet talk. Your dog won't learn a darned thing, but you might feel better!

• Secondly, a correction should be clear enough, and firm enough to interrupt what your pup is doing, but not something that terrifies or hurts your pup. "Remote" corrections only need to be startling, they *don't* need to frighten her to be effective, they just need to interrupt the behavior.

• Corrections should happen slightly before or just as the pup gets into trouble (just as she initiates the undesirable behavior). Just as quickly, you should be directing her toward an appropriate alternative behavior. Immediately redirect your pup with a toy, some cues like sit, down or come, or to another activity in another area. Remember, you are much better off teaching your pup what you DO want her to do, than correcting her for what you don't!

PRAISE & REINFORCEMENT

We've talked a bit about praise and reinforcement in Chapter 1, but they are so important that it is a good idea to talk about them in more depth. First off, now is a good time to ask yourself if your dog goes all happy and wiggly when you say "Good Dog." If not, you'd be smart to keep conditioning an association between something good (treat or play) and your praise words. Without it, "Good Dog" is no more effective than your boss saying "Smesh Blecka" to you—a meaningless sound that isn't going to cause you to feel appreciated. But if every time you heard "Smesh Blecka" you got a bonus, those sounds would make you very happy.

Here's how you can create an association between verbal praise and something good: Use words that are short and snappy so that you can get them out fast in a happy and friendly voice. Say "Good Dog" or "Yes" or "Wow"—

> . . . Immediately before giving him a treat (you can do this 5-10 times in a row for more effect).
>
> . . . As he enjoys his dinner.
>
> . . . While he's blissfully chewing on a favorite toy.
>
> . . . While he's getting a belly rub and loving it.

You get the idea: pair the praise with times that he feels happy, and eventually he'll automatically feel good when you say "Good" That gives you the ability to reinforce him whether you have a treat in your pocket or not, and to use the praise at the moment he did what you wanted. "Timing, timing, timing" is the dog training equivalent of real estate's "location, location, location." This is a good week to practice praising your dog the *instant* he does what you want. Follow up with the treat or toy, but get that praise in immediately so that he knows exactly what it was that led to the reinforcement.

CLICKER TRAINING Another effective way to tell your dog that he did something good is to use a handheld clicker. First you "load" the clicker to make it effective by clicking it and immediately giving your dog a treat. Repeat this, pairing up "click-treat," "click-treat" fifteen to twenty times, until your dog learns that the click means a treat is coming. You can usually do this in one or two sessions. Once your dog associates the click with a treat, you can use the clicker in place of praise. The advantages of a clicker are 1) it is precise: the sound snaps out abruptly and can be used to mark the exact behavior you were looking for and 2) it is consistent: you can say "Good Dog" many different ways, but the click will always sound exactly the same to your dog. That clarifies communication, and clarity is crucial when anyone, person or dog, is trying to learn something new. Clicker training can be a great way to communicate with your dog, and to allow your dog to think for himself about what action he should take to get you to make that clicking sound.

Keep reinforcing! A common mistake is to stop reinforcing too early in training.

Of course, the disadvantage is that you have to remember to have your clicker with you, but it is small and easy to put in your pocket. Some sound-sensitive dogs are put off by the click at first, but that can be overcome. Patricia held it behind her back or used it inside a pocket with some of her sound-sensitive Border Collies, and they quickly grew to love the sound.

KEEP REINFORCING One of the most common mistakes of novices is to stop reinforcing their dog too early in training. New owners tend to shower their pups with praise and treats early on, but then drop the reinforcements out as soon as they start to see a consistent response. However, good habits take a long time to establish but very little time to break down. That's what it's important to keep reinforcing your dog often, even though you vary the types of rewards your dog gets.

MANAGE THE DISTRACTION LEVEL Pay particular attention to the context in which you've asked your dog to perform. Sitting on cue in the kitchen when it's just you, your pup and a dinner bowl is profoundly different than sitting when company comes. Dogs, especially puppies, are easily overwhelmed by distractions—after all, there are a million things to do besides what you are asking. That means you need to be the most interesting game in town. Think of it as a competition—you're competing for your dog's attention with the rest of his environment—which includes other people, squirrels in the backyard, and riveting scents in the grass. Thus, you'll need your best reinforcements, like cooked chicken, when asking your dog to listen to you when he is distracted. Ones of lower value, like commercial dog treats, can be used when it's easier for him to pay attention.

Avoid asking a young dog to sit or come when called if he is overwhelmed with distractions. One of the biggest differences between professional trainers and novices is that the pros know when to keep their mouths shut. Did your pup just find a food wrapper on the floor? This is not the time to ask him to come. Go to your pup and lure him away with a treat, then call him to come once you have his attention. If you want your pup to sit at the door when cousin Harry and his five children come to visit, don't bother saying sit unless are right beside your dog with a piece of chicken in your hand.

Remember that young puppies don't have the emotional control of a mature dog. That's why you need to be thoughtful about when and where you ask your pup to do what you ask. If you want your dog to respond consistently, then you need to gradually work your way up to it. That means not calling him to come when he's in over his head. He's just a kid after all! We'll talk in Chapter 6 about what you can expect in his first year of life, but for now, do what you can to "set your pup up to win" by only asking him to comply when he is not overly distracted.

 # NEW EXERCISES

THE NAME GAME

Most dog owners don't go out of their way to teach a dog to respond to his name, yet what sound could be more important? If you want your dog to pay attention to what you say, you need a way to get his attention. If you think about it, that's what names are for—we say "Hey Marsha" or "John, could you…." as a way of letting another know we want them to listen to us.

However, there's no reason your dog should automatically take his attention off a chew toy or a smell in the grass just because you made a sound that you label a "name." That's why it is valuable to teach your pup early on that wonderful things will happen if he turns to look at you when you say his name. Go out of your way now to make him glad he responds to his name, and in a few months he'll automatically give you his attention every time you say it.

Start by having at least 15 to 25 extra tasty treats in your hand or training pouch, and move into an area in which your dog will be mildly distracted. (Don't set him up to fail by starting in an area where he is overwhelmed with too many sights, smells or sounds.) Wait for him to start sniffing the rug or looking elsewhere, and then say his name. If he turns his head toward you, immediately say "Good!" (or your own version of praise) and give him a treat. Then look up and walk a few feet forward, stop and look away from your puppy. If you take your attention off of him, he'll be more likely to take his attention off of you. Since the exercise is about changing his attention from the environment back to you, you need him looking away from you before you say his name. When he is looking elsewhere, say his name as before, and praise the instant his head turns toward you and give him another treat. Repeat that four or five times in a row, giving him more than one treat for especially impressive responses.

If you say his name and he doesn't turn his head, walk forward a few steps away from what's distracting him and try again. Once you've said his name, try as hard as you can to let him initiate the action without any more words or movements from you; if he initiates looking at you on his own he'll learn faster and be more consistent later on. If you have to, clap your hands or make smooching noises to help direct his attention toward you, but after a few repetitions, stop "helping" and give him a chance to do it on his own. Then be lightening fast with the treat to reward him when he does give you his attention.

A cautionary note: just about every human ever born tends to repeat the dog's name if the first iteration didn't work. Thus, a reasonable subtitle of this section could be: "Rocky? Rocky! ROCKY!!!" But if your response to inattention is to repeat the dog's name louder and louder, you're just teaching him to ignore you until the second or third repetition. This week, concentrate on saying your dog's name just once, and then moving to a new spot if it didn't work the first time. If you're not getting a good response, try working in a less distracting environment, and ensuring that Rocky knows you have treats in your hand. Play this game several times a day, varying when and where you ask him to look at you. Be mindful of the level of difficulty—don't get swept away by early successes and ask for him to turn away from high-level distractions yet. You always want to build on a foundation of success, so be sure to go one step at a time.

This week, notice how and when you say your dog's name in other contexts. Many of us (okay, all of us!) tend to say our dog's name often, but not necessarily in a way that is useful. Most commonly, we say "Coco" or "Laddie," and assume that through some miraculous process our dogs will know that what we *really* meant was "Coco come!" or "Lad, don't chew on the electric cord." But alas, mind-reading dogs have yet to be bred, and until that happens we need to go out of our way to ensure that we are effectively communicating what we want. Don't worry when you notice yourself saying your dog's name and nothing else, but make a mental note of it. After a few days, without consciously trying, you'll start letting your dog know why you wanted his attention, instead of just saying his name and expecting him to read your mind. At the same time, he'll magically become better behaved!

NO JUMPING UP

Dogs naturally jump up on people when they are young—they are trying to get near our faces and lick our mouths in order to greet us politely, like a proper dog should. When they are little, we think it's sweet and cute. When they are grown up, we think it's rude. Go figure. Of course, we add to their natural inclinations by reinforcing them for jumping up as puppies—we pet them and giggle with amusement when they do. It's no surprise then, that we have trouble when visitors come to the door!

This is the time to teach your pup that humans have our own way of greeting, and it involves keeping all of our feet on the floor. Begin by monitoring your own behavior. Are you reinforcing your puppy for jumping up? (And who doesn't without training themselves not to?) You can change that by being mindful: do what you can, benevolently, to avoid reinforcing your puppy when she jumps up. Don't correct her for it, just gently ask for a sit and then pet, praise or give a treat.

At the same time, help her out by having everyone ask for a brief sit when they greet her. As soon as she does, reinforce her by going down to her level and petting, praising or giving her a treat as she keeps all four paws on the ground. Ask her to sit often, so that she gets used to approaching a person and sitting down as she greets them. In the next chapter we'll add some exercises that will help her learn to keep "four on the floor on her own."

WALKING BY YOUR SIDE

It is natural for people to walk side-by-side together—very young children do it without us having to teach them how, because it is part of our own innate behavior. We want our dogs to do it too, but it doesn't come naturally to them. Heeling is as natural for puppies as calculus is for people. Think about the times you've been on a walk

Heeling is as natural for puppies as calculus is for people

with several dogs who were free to move around. Did they walk in pairs, shoulder to shoulder with one another? Hardly! They might join together over an interesting scent in the grass, or run side-by-side while playing, but most of their walking is done independently. That's why we have to teach dogs to walk beside us, moving at our walking pace, which must seem incredibly slow and boring to them. "Heeling," or even walking politely on a leash, is a lot more difficult for a dog than sitting on cue or lying down when asked. Here are two tips to help you and your dog enjoy your walks together: 1) Teach the "Follow Game" as a "Pre-Heel" exercise, and 2) Use the right equipment. We'll go over them one at a time.

THE FOLLOW GAME

When puppies are young they have a strong social attachment to their caregivers. You can use this to condition your pup to love being next to you as you walk. A more formal "heel" command should come later in life. For now, your objective should be to motivate your puppy to *want* to pay attention to you and walk by your side. However, no matter how charming you might be, there are lots of tempting and distracting things out there in the environment competing for your pup's attention, so you will need to be extra interesting to keep your pup focused on you.

Begin with your dog off leash (if it's 100% safe) in a quiet place that has few distractions. Have a handful of treats (a treat pouch that you attach to your belt is handy here), and show them to your dog. Once your pup looks interested in them, walk a few paces away. Don't lure your pup through space, just stand up and walk a few feet away, clapping your hands or smooching if necessary to get your pup's attention. If your pup keeps up with you and follows, praise and give her a treat.

Now walk a few steps in another direction, again giving your pup a treat as she catches up to you. Try to avoid her swinging around and getting a treat while facing you—that's going to make it difficult later on to give her a treat as she walks by your side. Give her the treat as she catches up and is facing the same way as you. If she doesn't follow, do what you need to do to encourage her to come to your side. Make smooching noises, clap your hands, wave the treat in the air or go back and show her the treat again until she catches up. However, don't call her to come—that's not going to teach her to initiate following you of her own accord.

After she has followed you for a few steps, give the treat as she gets to your side, then turn and take off in another direction. Don't go too far, she's just a puppy. If you get too far away you'll lose her attention. If you need to (but *only* if you need to) smooch, make a clicking sound with your tongue, or do something to get her attention in a fun, playful way. Once she catches up and is beside you, make sure she is really glad to be there.

Repeat this game just a few times and then quit while you are both still having lots of fun. Do it again later in the day. Practice this in your house or your yard, or for 30 seconds in the middle of a leash walk. Practice often throughout the day in little 10 second bursts. Be sure to try it often in unfamiliar places while she is still young. You'll make the biggest impression on her when you do it away from home where she may be a bit more concerned about "losing" you.

There are several keys to making this work well:
• Start where you can win. Don't do this where she'll be overwhelmed with distractions.

• Use lots of small, tasty treats to reinforce her for paying attention to you.

• Make your movements interesting: take two fast steps away from her, then treat and move in another direction. If you always walk in a straight line—well, how interesting is that?

PUT IT ON CUE You'll notice at this point we haven't put a word on this behavior yet. It's a good idea to get the behavior working fairly well before you "put it on cue." Once you can predict successfully that she'll follow you when you move away, you can start to use a verbal cue. Since you're working on attention and following rather than a formal heel, you might want to choose a casual title that means "stay close to me," and save the word "heel" for a more formal command later. (Heel traditionally defines a specific position with the dog's neck next to your left leg—not further ahead or behind by more than a couple inches. It's a much more precise, more advanced concept for her to learn.) Choose something that sounds very different from your other cues, perhaps "This Way" or "Let's Go!"

THE RIGHT TOOL FOR THE JOB Everyone's seen them – the 5 to 205 pound Suburban sled dogs – hauling their owners down the street from light post to fire hydrant. Maybe you have one yourself. If so, walking your dog isn't much fun, and that's not good for you or your dog. The problem isn't just a training issue; it's an equipment problem. After all, no one expects an untrained horse "heel" as it is led from the barn. You can't control an intractable horse with a lead rope attached to a "collar" around the base of their neck—in that case, physics would be on the side of the horse.[5] Indeed, the largest part of the harness that allows a horse to pull a wagon is the "collar." The horse pushes his chest forward into it, and the wagon, being attached, has to follow along. Dogs can use their collars in the same way. Add that to the fact that your dog's muscles work in opposition—as you pull one way, his muscles automatically pull the other—and you've got a tiny little dog who can haul you around like a draft horse.

The old-fashioned solutions to this problem involved using a "choke" or "training" collar that tightened continually the harder the dog pulled, or a "prong" collar with spikes that pressed into the dog's neck. Both of these methods can work for some individuals, but more often they either hurt or scare the dog, or simply don't work. Choke collars are especially ineffective, as dogs are amazingly resistant to increasing levels of pressure around their neck. Prong collars can hurt dogs and/or elicit defensive aggression. However, there are new products on the market that radically improve things for both people and dogs, finally getting

> *If your dog pulls you through the neighborhood, you probably have an equipment problem.*

---

5 There is a growing movement of people using positive reinforcement and an understanding of horse psychology to do just that. Yeah for them!

physics on your side so that you can walk side-by-side with your dog without being dragged around like a helpless victim.

Once your pup learns to walk at your side without pulling we advise using a buckle collar and a four to six-foot leash. But while you're working on that, you'd be wise to get the right tools for the job. One of the best pieces of equipment you can get is called a "front attachment body harness." Given what we just said about draft horses using harnesses to pull wagons, this recommendation might seem counter-intuitive, but these harnesses have the leash attached to the band that goes across *the front your dog's chest*, not at the top of the back. Thus, your dog can't sink his body forward and push against the chest band. The connection in the front allows you to steer and control your dog, while preventing him from pushing his chest against the harness and pulling against you. Most dogs accept these harnesses without a sniff, seeming to be perfectly comfortable with them from the moment they are first fitted. There are several brands on the market, including the original, SENSE-ation™ harness by Softouch Concepts and the Easy Walk™ Harness by Premier.

Another good solution for extra large or exuberant puppies is the "head collar." One brand, the Gentle Leader,™ was the first effective and humane solution to walking a dog who was more interested in chasing a chipmunk than walking beside you on the sidewalk. Head collars look like the halters on horses, and allow you to control your dog's actions by controlling where his head is facing. When you pull on the leash the dog's nose and his eyes are directed toward you. Dogs tend to think about what they're looking at, so once you have your dog looking at you, you're likely to have his attention as well. Head collars work beautifully for some dogs. However, some dogs aren't as crazy about them as their owners are, and spend much of the time trying to paw them off. You might try the front-attached harness first, and move up to head collar if need be. If you do use a head collar, avoid making sudden, hard tugs on the leash, and don't use them with long lines or retractable leashes. You don't want your dog's neck injured if his head snaps around abruptly. This is easy to avoid if you use them correctly.

Keep in mind that all these devices are management tools, and aren't substitutes for good training. Once trained and matured, many dogs will walk beside you happily and politely on a simple buckle collar and a loose leash. In an ideal world, that would be true for all dogs. But every dog is different, and some dogs will always be a little bit more challenging than others. There's no reason not to use a harness or head collar for the rest of your dog's life if it works out best for both of you.

PRACTICE MAKES PERFECT

SIT-DOWN-STAND REVISITED

If you've been practicing these cues with your pup, he should be doing them reliably most of the time, IF there are no distractions. If that's the case, use treats only some of the time, substituting praise, toys, and chest rubs for food when practicing these commands in familiar places with few distractions. If it's not, continue using treats as much as you needed to get the right response. Keep in mind that most pups learn to sit on cue fastest, followed by stand and then lie down. That's especially true when they are distracted—lying down being the last thing they want to do if they see another dog across the street.

CONSCIOUSLY INCREASE THE LEVEL OF DISTRACTION If things are going well, start asking your puppy to respond in the midst of mild to moderate distractions. Some things that can be considered mild distractions are: practicing outside instead of inside; training with the cat waiting by the doorway; or practicing with new people watching. It's amazing how small a change can throw things off, so remember that any noise, movement, smell, presence of others, or change of location can be considered a distraction. We wouldn't expect a puppy who has been practicing quietly in the house without the cat around to "down" while two cats chase each other through the room! Your dog will eventually get to that point, but you will need to help him get there step-by-step. Don't expect your puppy to jump from step 2 to step 25 without working up to it gradually. If you don't think there's an 80% chance your pup will respond correctly, then at this stage, don't ask!

CONTINUE SEPARATING YOUR VERBAL AND VISUAL CUES Especially with sit and stand, continue to practice using each type of signal by itself. Some pups are much faster than others at responding to your voice alone, so don't worry if your pup seems to need you to link a visual cue with the sound you make. But be aware that you need to consciously work on saying the word while not moving—otherwise the move you made earlier as a "lure" becomes the only relevant cue to your dog. Once you get the hang of it, it is easy to only give one cue at a time, but it requires paying as much attention to what *you're* doing as you are to what your pup is doing. A great way to compare your behavior with your dog's responses is to have someone video tape you while you are training your dog. Try it for the whole family, and then compare everyone's actions for an illustrative exercise in human behavior. This is a great "teachable" moment for the whole family, and a wonderful way to introduce children to the study of behavior, and how their behavior affects that of others.

COME REVISITED

Practice "come"...*always*!! Continue to make it a fun game. Call your puppy to you often, then immediately release her to go do something else fun. Remember not to call your pup for things she perceives as bad. That's a surefire way to teach her *not* to come. Take advantage of the times when she is racing joyously to you of her own accord (you just got the leash out of the closet; you're pulling her "lost" toy out from under the couch, etc.). Call "come" just before she starts to head your way. However, don't call her to come too many times in a row. Call her once or twice (3 or 4 times at the most), and always *make it worth her while*, then quit. Do this several times a day, in different locations indoors and out, on leash and, when it's safe, off leash.

A WORD TO THE WISE Only use your "come" cue when you are willing to go and get your pup if she doesn't come. Take it from us, that is easier said than done! It seems that we humans can barely stop ourselves from calling come when we're not ready to ensure that it happens. We tend to call come once, and then stand still, repeatedly calling "Come" while our pup is enthralled in some major distraction. If she's rolling in her first cow pie, what do you think the chances are that she'll leave it to come to you? About zero! So don't call her to "come" when you know she's not going to do it. Otherwise she'll just learn to ignore you while you rattle off "Come puppy, come, come, come" while she heads the other way. She's too young to be reliable at this age.

Instead, go get her. If she doesn't come, don't punish her or reel her in like a fish on a line, but do be persistent and interesting enough to draw her attention back onto you. Don't let her learn that she can ignore your request. Quietly walk up to her, and call, clap, whistle, laugh, squeak, smooch, play bow, and/or wave a piece of food (then put it back in your pocket, you're using it here only to get her attention). Once you have her attention, take off running! Move! Find some way to get her attention onto you, and get her to follow you, if only for a couple of feet. Then give her something better than what she just left, such as a great treat or an invigorating chase game. Better yet, if at all possible, release her and let her go back to the distraction she just left—that way she won't associate coming when called with the end of her fun. (Hey, you're going to have to bathe her anyway, you might as well get some heavy duty training leverage out of that disgusting cow pie incident!)

Begin to add some mild distractions when you call her to come, but build the distractions up gradually.

Begin to add some mild distractions when you call her to "come," but build up your distraction level gradually. You want her to learn to pay attention to you when other things are going on, but you don't want to lose her attention altogether. And you *will* lose her attention if you expect too much of her too quickly. Instead, add distractions a bit at a time. If what you added was too much for her, and you completely lost her attention, try again with fewer distractions and better reinforcements. Then try going back to your original distraction, but call her from a much shorter distance away, giving her a lot more help and encouragement this time around.

For example, your dog might be great at coming in the house when the two of you are alone in the living room, but it's an entirely different matter to come away from a chattering squirrel in the backyard. The latter is so distracting that no young dog should be expected to come just to your voice if you are twenty feet away. Rather, go all the way to your dog with a treat in your hand if she is enraptured by a distraction. Show her the treat and lure her partway to you, then call her to come all the way. A middle step would be to call her to come from the backyard when there was nothing special going on.

I LOVE IT WHEN YOU GRAB MY COLLAR This is also a great time to condition your pup that it's fun to have someone reach for and take a hold of her collar. So often owners take a dog by the collar to drag them somewhere they don't want to go, teaching the dog to shy away from someone reaching toward them. That can be a disaster when a good Samaritan tries to help catch a lost or loose dog.

To avoid your pup shying away from an outstretched hand:
• Avoid using her collar to move her from A to B. Use treats and toys and your own movements to encourage her to go where you want. If you have to use her collar, attach her leash to it and use it to move her to where she needs to go.

• Add "collar touches" to your come game. About ten percent of the time that you call her to come, ask her to sit when she arrives. When she gets to you, reach out and hold her collar for one second, saying "Good girl, Good girl." Give her a treat with the other hand, and then release the collar and initiate something fun. The idea is to teach her that it's fun when people take a hold of her collar, and that nothing bad will happen if they do. Remember to only do this part of the time: asking for a sit every time you call is perceived as punishment by some dogs.

For all the cues that you're working on right now, remember that your puppy will learn best from repeated successes. It's good to stretch the envelope a bit and make your requests a bit more challenging for her, but, most importantly, help her to succeed. At this stage, your dog is *in training*, she's not "trained" to come when called yet, no matter what the distraction!

SUMMARY

• Be sure you have conditioned your dog to feel good when you praise him. Do that by linking praise with treats, by praising as you rub him behind the ears and as he eats his dinner, etc. Remember that good habits take a long time to solidify; reinforce your puppy generously for good behavior with praise, treats, pets and play, especially at this young age.

• Respond to problem behaviors (like inappropriate chewing) by managing the environment to prevent problems, redirecting your pup to an appropriate behavior (always ask yourself: "What DO I want my dog to be doing right now?") and teaching a cue that means "Please stop doing that, we don't do that here!"

• Avoid physical corrections and ignore advice that you have to "dominate" your dog. Teach your pup what you'd like him to do, and discourage what you don't want through management and re-direction.

• Play the Name Game, and teach your pup that it is in his best interest to pay attention when you say his name.

• Begin teaching your pup to keep "four-on-the-floor" by asking him to sit as you approach, and then squatting down to greet and pet him. Ask friends to help out by asking for a sit as they approach too.

If he jumps up at this age, just ask for a sit before you pet or praise.

• Start off your pup's leash manners by playing the Follow Game. Go outside with some treats in your pocket, choosing a place that is relatively quiet. Show the treats to your dog, then turn away and walk a few feet from your dog. If your pup follows you, praise and treat. Continue moving a few steps away from him, and treating every time he catches up to you. Try to treat him as he is parallel to you, before he swings around to the front as if to sit.

• Continue practicing sit, down, stand and come. Gradually increase the distraction level, but be sure you have a high-quality reinforcement when you do. If you call come and get no response, don't repeat the word, but walk closer to your pup and lure him in your direction with a food treat. Praise and treat after he moves a few steps toward you, and then call him to come again, when you are much closer.

4
PLAY! PLAY! PLAY!

★ SPECIAL TOPIC

PLAY

What is more fun than watching a puppy play? It seems so joyful and free—surely it's one of the pleasures of getting a puppy (and why all that work on housetraining is worth it). But the frolicsome nature of play has a serious side, because play can be the making of a perfect dog, or the road to serious trouble. We'll start with all the ways that play can enhance the bond between you and your pup, and help you raise a dog who is a joy to live with.

Puppies love to play as much as we love to watch them doing it, and that's why it is so valuable as a training tool. You can use play as a highly effective reinforcement, and at the same time use it to help your dog learn boundaries and emotional control. Combining play with simple cues like sit or come helps to motivate your puppy and keeps her interested in what you are doing. Professional trainers often use play to produce reliable results when training dogs for the Obedience ring, Schutzhund, or Search and Rescue work. Even police dogs are trained to a very high level of reliability using play as the motivating factor. Don't underestimate the power of play as a motivator to produce a well-mannered family dog that is happy to do what you ask.

Play also gives you an opportunity to teach manners in a fun, positive way that makes life much more fun for you and your dog. For example,

Play while training and train while playing!

imagine what might happen after your dog picks up something she shouldn't have. You could yell "NO!" in a loud angry voice and run at her to grab it out of her mouth, or you could say "Drop It!" in a happy voice, *if* she's learned that "Take It/Drop It" is a great game. The former often leads to a dog who learns to run away and play "Catch Me If You Can!" (a favorite of many canines), while the latter leads to a dog dropping the object and happily trotting over to you to see what wonderful things are going to happen next.

There's yet another reason to incorporate play into your pup's training: All polite members of society, whether two-legged or four, need to learn to manage their level of emotional arousal. That's why we have playground monitors at schools, because young children can become caught up in the excitement of play, and start to get into trouble. That's one of the advantages of sports—they provide boundaries to contain our behavior. When children play games like softball, they have to learn how to play within the rules and they have to learn to moderate their excitement or disappointment when things don't go as they'd like. Puppies are like children—they don't seem to mind learning the rules if they enjoy the game. Here are some ideas to get the two of you started.

> *Use some of these games to exercise both your pup's mind and body.*

 NEW EXERCISES

TAKE IT and DROP IT

The advantages of teaching this to your pup as a game are obvious: no chasing after your pup with the remote control in her mouth, no adolescent dog hiding under the bed growling at you with a chicken wing in his mouth! But, of course, you have to first take the time to teach Drop It, and here's how:

Start by arming yourself with some great treats in your pocket and a toy that is big enough for both you and your pup hold onto at the same time. Rope toys work especially well, but make sure it is a toy that your dog likes to play with. Keep your hand on one end of the toy while you present the other end to your pup. Wiggle the toy in front of her (not too close or you'll chase her away!) to entice her to grab it and say "Take It" just as her mouth closes around the toy. Maintain your own hold of the other end of the toy, and play a short game of tug with her, pulling back just enough to keep her engaged.

After a few seconds of playing tug, say "Drop It" as you move a small, tasty treat to her nose with your other hand. Don't let go of the toy. If the food is good enough, she'll spit out the toy to take the food. As she opens her mouth, praise her and pop the food in her mouth as reinforcement for dropping the object. If you can, repeat this a few times in one session. Some dogs don't allow for repeats, because once they know you have a bag of treats they lose interest in the toy. That's okay, just try it again a little bit later.

The idea here is to teach your dog that Drop It is just one part of a fun game. Drop It is the flip side of Take It, and always leads to something good happening. For now, it's important to guard against using "Drop It" functionally. Don't use it when you discover your pup picking up something she shouldn't have. She hasn't mastered it yet, and she needs more practice before she can do it when it's hard for her to comply. In Chapter 5 we'll go over the steps that will lead to using Drop It when you really need it.

FETCH

THE BEST GAME IN TOWN Fetch is an absolutely wonderful game for you and your dog. Once your dog knows this game, you can give him lots of physical and mental exercise—while you stand still. There are many ways to teach this all-time favorite game. The first method we'll describe is for dogs who already show some interest in a ball (or other toy) and will pick it up in their mouths.

The first rule to this game, whatever method you use, is the hardest one: *Don't let your dog teach YOU to fetch for him.* "Ha Ha!" you say, "that'll never happen." Except it does, more often than not, because dogs love the "Tag I'm It Game" and are great trainers, being far more patient and consistent than we humans. So here's the most important part of fetch training: your dog should always move toward you, while you rarely move toward your dog.

That said, try starting in an area with few distractions. Pick up one of your dog's favorite toys, (a ball in this example) and use movement to attract his attention by wiggling the ball one or two feet in front of him. As he orients toward the ball and gets excited about it, toss it 2 to 3 feet away, no more. It's important not to toss it too far away at first, especially when working with young dogs.

As your puppy runs over to the ball, remain silent to avoid distracting him. Wait until his mouth closes around the ball, and then begin clapping and running *away* from him. Don't use his name or call him to come—he'll be more likely to drop the ball if you do. Use handclaps and your movement to attract your puppy toward you. As he gets to you with the ball in his mouth, resist the urge to move toward him with your arm outstretched. If you lean forward, he'll lean away, and notice that moving away from you makes you move closer to him. Yipee! Now he's figured out how to get you to chase him! Better to wait for him to drop the ball. Turn away from him if he teases you with it—playing hard to get works with dogs too.

If he drops the ball on the way back to you, (a very common response) go ahead and pick it up and throw it again. That was a great response after all—he chased after the ball, picked it up, brought it part way back and dropped it. Good boy! Throw it for him again, and gradually, over the months, hold out for better and better retrieves before throwing the ball, using chases (remember, only he chases you!), smooches and hand claps to get him closer to you.

If he gets all the way to you but won't give up the ball, turn away from him as though you aren't interested in his silly ball. Fold your arms, turn and walk a few feet away. Most dogs will follow you and try to get your attention on the ball. When he finally drops the ball, pick it up and *throw it instantly.* The most common mistake people make when trying to teach fetch is not throwing the ball *the instant* the dog releases it. They ask him to sit, they pet him on the head, they say pretty words to him when all of that just frustrates him. All he wants is to get the ball back, so don't hoard it, throw it!

EASY DOES IT You'll have the most luck teaching your pup to fetch if you keep your sessions extremely short at first. Try only two or three tosses, and then end the game before he tires of it. If he brings the ball back three times in a row, and then loses interest, just turn around and walk away. Game over. If he is predictable, becoming less reliable around the 4th or 5th toss for example, just end the game after two or three tosses. This is common in young dogs; it takes most dogs a good year to consistently play the game the way we want them to play, so be patient. And remember, it's just a game!

I BROUGHT IT BACK, BUT I'M NOT GIVING IT UP! Some dogs will bring the ball all the way back to you, but keep their jaws clamped around it no matter what you do. They want to play ball, oh yes they do, but they want you to chase them. If you can't get out of this scenario, try this:

Start with two objects, preferably identical objects (such as two tennis balls). Begin as described previously: wiggle the ball and toss it a couple feet away. As he picks it up, clap and run backwards. But this time, as your pup approaches, bring the second ball out of your pocket and start waving it around, tossing it in the air and catching it yourself.

Your little ball thief will most likely become interested in the ball you have because it's moving and you have it and he doesn't. That makes it almost irresistible. He'll most probably drop the first ball at some point and focus on the second ball that you are still holding. As he does, throw the second ball to reinforce the behavior you wanted, (him dropping the first ball). You'd be wise to throw the second ball behind you, so that he comes racing up to you and past you to get the second ball, rather than learning to stop short before he gets to you with the first one.

While he's busy chasing the second ball, quietly go pick up the first one and start teasing him with the ball you just picked up. Repeat this sequence, but only do this 2 or 3 times in a row at most, then quit. Just once will be enough for some dogs. It's important to stop the game while the puppy still wants more; you can always play again later if he seems interested.

BALL? WHAT BALL? Some dogs won't put a toy or ball in their mouths at all, much less fetch it. They won't even follow the ball's movement with their eyes. In this case, use a toy that you can smear with food. Use some wonderful food that your dog adores, like canned dog or cat food, liver sausage, peanut butter, etc. As he licks the toy it will move a bit and he may begin to mouth it to get the food off. Put more food on or in it, and toss it just a foot or two in front of him. This time he should track the movement of the ball with his eyes because he knows it has food on it. He'll probably trot over to lick off the food. If he (eventually) picks it up off the floor, cheer and clap and make a really big deal out of this important step he's taken. Give him an even better piece of food for picking the toy up in his mouth. Gradually increase the distance that you throw the toy, and gradually reduce the use of food on the toy. Many dogs can eventually be enticed to retrieve with this method, but it does take some patience.

CATCH

It's always fun to have a dog that catches things you throw up in the air. Begin by tossing food at your pup's nose from two to three feet away. After a bit of trial and error, he'll begin to track its path with his eyes, and then try to catch it. It takes practice to catch something, whether it's with your mouth or your hands, so don't laugh at him (too much!) when the treat hits him in the face. Once he begins to catch most of the treats you toss from a short distance, you can begin to increase the distance and even put a cue word on it if you'd like. Say "Catch" just before you toss the treat. As he gets the hang of it you can start tossing soft toys to him.

FLYING DISCS AND PUPPIES

You may be ready to teach your dog to catch flying objects, and why not? It can be a great game for both of you. However, it does have its drawbacks. Veterinarians see a lot of injuries associated with flying disc play. They tell us they see a lot of broken and cracked teeth from hard objects, so it's essential to use a soft object made especially for dogs. (Frisbee®, and many other companies, make soft discs just for dogs.) Vets also see injuries from dogs jumping up and twisting to catch the disc and then landing in abnormal positions, putting undue strain on various parts of the body. This is especially problematic when your pup is growing and developing, don't play this type of game with your pup without first talking to your veterinarian.

WHERE'S JOHN?

This is a great way to keep your puppy busy, both mentally and physically, and it's a fun game for the kids to play with a puppy. Begin with two or more people standing about 10 to 15 feet apart, facing each other. The first person (we'll call her Kathy) asks the pup, "Where's John?" At that instant John calls the pup while clapping and bending down to attract the puppy towards him.

When the pup arrives, John makes a big fuss over how brilliant she is, and gives her a treat. Then John asks, "Where's Kathy?" and at that instant Kathy calls the pup, just as John did. Kathy gets all silly and excited when the puppy gets to her, running away so the pup can chase her a little bit, or giving the puppy a belly rub to make her glad she found Kathy.

Repeat this sequence back and forth a few times, but be sure to quit while the puppy is still excited about the game. You don't want her to get bored with it. Next time you practice, begin to increase the distance between the people. Work your way up to being in separate rooms, or behind separate trees when you're outside.

As your pup begins to catch on to the game, have one person send the puppy without the second person calling the pup. Now your

Keep your puppy mentally and physically exercised by teaching "Where's John?"

pup should be running to find the other person just because you said "Where's ....?" Most pups catch on to this first part of the game pretty quickly.

The second phase of this game is to ensure that the pup truly associates the words spoken with the name of the individual. Often, at this point, especially if you've only played with two people, your pup has learned to run a pattern back and forth, finding whichever person isn't present at the moment. That means they don't necessarily associate the sound "Kathy" with a particular person. You could say "Where's the Giraffe?" and they'd run to the person who is farthest away.

To help her learn to distinguish between various names, it helps to have 3 or 4 people for the pup to run between. Begin in a large circle (maybe 10-20 feet in diameter) and have one send the pup to another, clearly using their name. If the pup goes to the wrong individual, that person ignores the pup completely, while the right one starts clapping and calling the pup. When the pup does go to the person who matches the name, she gets lots of praise and reinforcement for coming, then is sent to the next person. If the puppy goes to the wrong person she gets ignored, and the target person calls to her. Through practice and repetition your pup can learn to distinguish between the names of each person in the group, then you can start to teach her names of other people as well. Just think, maybe someday your friend Timmy will fall down the well, and your dog will save his life when someone says "Where's Timmy?" (And then you could have your own television show.)

FIND THE TOY

Teaching your pup to find a specific toy is a similar process to "Where's John?" except that the toy won't be able to call him! Start by teasing your pup just a bit with a favorite toy and then "hide" it close by in full view, only a few feet away. Say "Find It! and encourage him to search it out; helping him if he needs it. Once he finds it, get silly-excited, as if he's done something wonderful, and let him play with it for a while. Try that two or three times in a row, again being careful to not bore him at this young age by trying to play for too long a time.

As the days go on, hide the toy a little farther away, perhaps in the next room, but partially visible through the door. Gradually make the hiding places harder to find. Many dogs begin by using their eyes, but as the weeks progress and you make the game harder, they'll start using their noses. Now you have a wonderful way to engage your pup's mind and body, and to keep him busy while you multi-task and watch television or pay bills. This is a wonderful, too-little-used game that can keep your pup busy when it's brutally cold outside, when you're cooking dinner or wanting to learn more about how your dog uses his nose to explore the world around him. It's a great game to play outside too—Patricia uses it in the yard on a daily basis with her young Border Collie who has physical limitations and can't do much running after toys outside.

BELLY UP (PLAY DEAD) & ROLL OVER

The classic "play dead" trick is a fun behavior to teach your pup and it has a practical side as well. You can use it when you need to groom your dog's belly, or when the veterinarian needs to examine your pup. Besides, it's really cute! To teach "belly up":

Begin with your pup in the "down" position on a soft, comfortable surface. Using a smelly, tasty treat, lure your pup's nose *slowly* around toward her side, so that her head moves in a semi-circle and she is looking partway toward her tail. Give her a treat in that position and let her move back to her usual posture. Start again, but this time move the treat closer to her tail, and treat again as her head turns a little bit more toward her hind end. In incremental steps, continue to lure her head around toward her tail, and then upward and backward over the top of her hip. If it's going well you'll notice her top foreleg starting to rise as her head goes back and around. Treat as soon as that leg goes up, and then continue to lure a little further back and over her hip until her own momentum tips her over onto her back. (This will make more sense when you try it!)

The key is to give her lots of treats for each incremental movement that is a bit closer to the one you eventually want. The most common mistake of a novice is to try to get a finished product before giving a treat. Give her a treat for every few inches she moves closer to the goal, and remember to keep it light hearted. It's a trick after all!

To teach "Roll Over," continue as above, but keep luring her nose all the way around in a semi-circle until she rolls all the way over. If her head follows the lure, her body will follow and she should flip over into a complete "roll over." Give the treat just as she flops over into the finished position. Be sure to do this in an area where she feels comfortable and relaxed—dogs are not happy to lie on their backs and expose their bellies if they are even a tad bit anxious, so try this in a quiet, comfy place.

HANDLING EXERCISES

"Opening My Dog's Mouth!" isn't a common game, but it pays off to teach your dog that handling exercises can be fun. Think of all the things you are going to have to do to protect your dog's health: open his mouth to see if something is stuck inside or to look at his gums, pull burrs out of his tail and clip his nails, to name a few. We'll grant that you're not going to convince a dog that having his nails trimmed is more fun than playing ball, but if you start early and do it right, you can avoid all kinds of grief down the road.

It's simple, if you start by thinking of grooming as a game yourself. For example, wait until your dog is lying down, and then sit down beside him with the nail clippers in hand. Give him a treat, then lure him into lying on his side, as described in Belly Up. Gently run your hand from his hip to his back foot, and pick up the foot, while giving him a treat with the other hand. Put the foot down, wait a second and pick it up again. As you hold his paw, give him another treat, and then clip off one tiny, TINY, minuscule sliver at the tip of one nail. (Are we clear here that this piece of nail should be microscopically small?) Say "Good Boy" and give another treat, then walk away. The message is: Treats come when clippers come, treats leave when clippers leave. (If necessary, have your vet or groomer teach you how to clip nails without slicing into the quick.) It's critical here not to overdo this: gentle handling can turn into harassment relatively fast, so engage in these exercises for only a minute or two, no more. Do your best to end on a good note, so that your pup wishes you'd keep it up rather than hoping you'll stop and leave him alone.

Incorporate the same step-by-step techniques for other handling exercises. Show your dog a treat and open his mouth briefly, then pop the treat into his mouth while it's still open. Pretend to pull a burr out of his tail by lying him down, gently pulling on a hank of hair on his tail and then give him a treat. Stay upbeat, as if this was a fun game, but don't be so enthusiastic that you hype your dog up so much that he can't stay still.

BACKYARD AGILITY

Negotiating obstacles that require climbing, balancing, tunneling, walking on unfamiliar surfaces, or limited jumping can help develop your pup's coordination, balance, problem-solving abilities, perseverance and confidence. Wow. That's a lot!

You don't need special equipment to practice agility at home.

You don't need special agility equipment for your puppy to practice these skills. Find things to challenge your pup's ability in the course of your normal day. For example: your pup could climb over a small log during your walk in the woods, or crawl under the coffee table or chair while you lure her with a toy. She could climb up and down stairs, go through a cardboard box you've opened on both ends, sit on a table (well, maybe not your antique maple one), or "jump" through a hula hoop you've suspended a few inches above the ground.

Just look around you and you'll find all sorts of opportunities to help your pup develop confidence in herself and trust in you through agility exercises. Keep safety in mind however. Be cautious about letting your pup do too much jumping or twisting while she is young. If she does jump, keep the heights very low. Repeated jumping can be hard on her developing bones and joints. Check with your veterinarian if you have questions about what activities are safe for your puppy.

TUG

This used to be a controversial subject, but most trainers now advise owners to teach tug games to their dogs, as long as they follow some basic rules. We agree that tug can be a great way to exercise your dog— it's sure a lot more fun playing tug games in the living room than it is taking your dog on a walk when it's sleeting outside. Tug games are also a great way to teach emotional control (for your dog, you're on your own yourself!). Dogs seem to love this game as much as we do, and we love that no one has to teach a dog to tug on an object.

However, you can also get your dog into trouble with tug games, so it's important that you both play by the rules. Dogs can get highly aroused playing tug, and behave in all sorts of inappropriate ways, just like human sports fans can when they lose emotional control. Keep the following in mind, and tug games can become a wonderful part of your relationship with your dog for years to come:

• Use "Take It/Drop It" when you play tug (see pages 60 and 89). You can even use tug games to teach a dog to drop an object on cue. Playing a few seconds of tug and then asking your dog to "Drop It" helps your dog learn to moderate her arousal levels.

• Speaking of arousal, tug games can be extremely exciting to dogs. To do them safely, you need to monitor your dog's level of arousal. If she starts biting higher and higher up the object, or starts looking as if she can no longer control herself, stop pulling back and become still and quiet. Then ask her to drop the toy, take a breather, and then start again. Keep in mind that dogs play with other dogs by interspersing high intensity play with lots of pauses. It seems that this is one way they prevent themselves from becoming overly excited. You'd be wise to incorporate similar pauses into play with your own dog.

• Don't worry about your dog growling when playing tug games with you! Growls by themselves are a normal part of tug games. Do stop the game, however, if your dog goes stiff, stares at your face and begins to growl—that's not play, it's a warning.

• Use appropriate toys—long ones that allow you to grip the toy a good foot away from your dog's mouth.

• Avoid whipping the toy back and forth as hard as you can. This might seem unfair, since that's exactly what your dog is going to do to you, but then, you don't have the toy in your mouth (one hopes). Because dogs use their necks to buffer the side-to-side action, they can be injured or strained if you use too much force when shaking the toy from side-to-side. Let your dog shake his head back and forth, but you should pull backwards, not sideways.

• Most children shouldn't be allowed to play tug with dogs. Kids aren't able to monitor their dog's arousal levels—they have enough of a challenge managing their own emotions.

• We used to advise that owners should always end up with the toy themselves once they're done playing, but research suggests that who "wins" has no bearing on the relationship between a dog and an owner. (However, super playful dogs were a bit pushier about demanding attention if they'd been allowed to keep the tug toy once the game was over. Only you know if this might apply to you and your dog!)

WHEN PLAY BACKFIRES

Puppies learn a lot about how to behave through their play, and so play can be your best friend, or your worst enemy. As Karen London and Patricia wrote in Play Together, Stay Together:

"Play is fun, but don't be fooled into thinking it's just goofy or frivolous. Play is powerful stuff, and it has a profound influence on your relationship with your dog."

Here is what you need to know about play to avoid future problems because of the games you play with your dog today.

SORRY, NO WRESTLING OR SLAPPING!

Dogs begin life playing with their littermates as if they are toys; they bite, wrestle, chase, pounce and chew on their brother and sisters just as we expect them to play with objects. We human primates like to get down and wrestle too—especially guys (with all due respect, it's primarily a guy thing). However, we've seen that wrestle play (called "rough and tumble wrestle play" by biologists) can cause serious problems between people and dogs. Often, a person ends up getting bitten and a dog ends up getting in trouble, if not put down or given away. Granted some people play this way with their dogs and never have a problem, but then, some people play Russian Roulette and win. Some don't.

The primary problem gets back to arousal levels, and the recognition that most play behaviors are the same actions that are used in fighting or predation. If a dog becomes overly aroused, or misinterprets an action from a human playmate, things can escalate into aggression in a heartbeat. Another potential problem is that play is sometimes used by dogs as a way of measuring social status. It is controversial how relevant this is to their relationships with people, but the fact is that there are a lot of subtle interactions between dogs that we probably don't even notice. How are we to know how they interpret our behavior when we're down on the ground with them?

If you think about it, wrestling or roughhousing games encourage biting and snapping at people. After all, inhibited bites are an essential part of play between dogs. But we aren't dogs, and our dogs need to learn to play with us in different ways than they play with one another. Be especially concerned about anyone playing "slap the face" games. That will teach your dog to snap at any hand approaching their face; not the best behavior to condition if you want to your dog around for a long and happy life.

Sometimes, training and behavioral problems can be traced back to roughhousing play with people. Does your pup persistently nip at your ankles as you walk out of the room? Does he jump up from behind and "tag" you with his teeth, because he's trying to get a game started? Are you having a hard time getting him to inhibit his bite and decrease his mouthing on people? These are common behaviors of many puppies, even ones whose owners have been model puppy raisers, but if these problems persist you might want to look at how each individual in the family is playing with the dog.

STAY AWAY FROM KEEP AWAY

Dogs try desperately to get us to chase them; they love a good chase and they especially love it if they are the chasee. But if we chase our pups around (at all) they quickly learn to play "keep away." This includes playing keep away when we call them to come, or when they've "stolen" something they shouldn't have. Obviously, we don't want that, especially if we're late for work and our puppy is heading off to Timbuktu. Here's how to avoid having your puppy play Keep Away when you're not in the mood:

Most importantly, don't chase after your puppy, and don't let other members of your family do so either. Granted this is sometimes easier said than done, but if you have to go get your puppy, do it as quietly as possible. If you want your puppy to come to you, you are much better off clapping to get her attention, and then running *away* from her. Now there's a chase game, but it's going in the right direction.

Remember, if you can't catch your pup or she won't come when you call, don't reinforce her by chasing after her. Instead make yourself interesting: run away, rattle the treat bag, toss a ball in the air, or roll in a cow pie for all we care, but don't chase after your dog! If you must go get her (and sometimes, for the sake of safety, you really must), then follow her quietly, moving only as fast as necessary to get to her side. If possible, get her attention with treats or an object (a stick on the ground? a tissue from your pocket?) and lure her in the direction you want to go. If you have nothing with you that is competitive with what's holding her attention, quietly snap the leash onto her collar and move her away. If you have one, give her a treat once she's headed in the right direction… you still want her to be glad she "came," even if it wasn't voluntarily.

Don't chase after your puppy, and don't let other members of your family do it either.

STEALING

PREVENTION PREVENTION PREVENTION Sorry to be so repetitive, but the fact is, dogs are natural born thieves. It's a trait that served their ancestors well, but we often find it to be inconvenient and annoying, not to mention potentially dangerous. The most important thing you can do is acknowledge that your pup is going to want to pick up objects and take them away, so that he can enjoy them in peace. That means you need to pro-actively prevent this from becoming a bad habit, by attending to your own behavior first.

Start by *puppy proofing* the entire house, moving tempting objects out of your dog's reach. Be sure to make dangerous electric cords inaccessible, either by encasing them in tubes or spraying them with a bitter substance on a daily basis. Even after you've done that, you need to actively supervise the pup to preempt any attempts on her part to steal unauthorized items.

Exercise is also an important part of prevention. Many dogs don't steal until they get bored and have excess energy to burn (which pretty much describes all healthy puppies who aren't asleep.) That's why exercise and the games above are so important for you and your puppy. Tire out her body, tire out her mind, and she'll be less likely to parade into the dining room, showing off your underwear to your dinner guests.

UH OH! SHE'S GOT THE REMOTE CONTROL! If your puppy does get something she shouldn't have (change that to "When your puppy....."), resist the temptation to go chasing after her. She'll only learn to play "keep away" as a wonderful new game and she'll have been reinforced for stealing. Then she'll be that much more likely to do it in the future.

When she has an item that you must get back right away, use a distraction to get her to drop it on her own. Rattle the treat bag, go get her leash, or begin playing with a ball by yourself. Pretend that you don't even notice there is a dog around, but that you just happen to be doing something terrific without her. Be fascinating; catch her attention in some way that entices her to come see what you're up to. If what you are doing is appealing enough, she will either drop her "prize" somewhere on her way over to you, or come over with the stolen item in her mouth. Once she comes over to get in the game, ask her to "Sit." If needed, you can put a piece of food near her nose to encourage her to drop her prize, saying "Drop It" as she opens her mouth to get the treat. But don't give her the food right away, make her work for it. Ask her to sit or down a few times, so she doesn't think you are rewarding her for stealing.

Once she has worked for your attention, then you can reward her sit or down, or divert her onto another activity while you quietly and unobtrusively repossess the stolen object. Then it's your job to prevent your pup from stealing it again through puppy proofing and careful management.

STAY OUT OF TROUBLE Avoid situations in which you reach in to grab things away from your puppy as she hides under a table or in a corner. The last thing you want to do is teach her to be defensive about possessions and wary of hands reaching toward her. Instead, ignore her and do something distracting to catch her attention so that she comes out on her own. Battling over possessions now can lead to more serious situations as your pup matures. If she has no interest in coming out, base your response on what she has. If it's not valuable and couldn't hurt her, ignore her and make a note to block the area with boxes in the future so that she can't get inside that area to hide. If the object valuable is valuable or dangerous, get it back as gently and quietly as possible. Don't yell, don't scold, just get the object back as undramatically as you can. If you can, lift the table or the chair so that you take away their hiding place. You may be angry—we've been there, honest—but scolding at this point won't prevent her from picking up a "treasure" again. It will, however, make her less likely to give it up in the future, and more likely to become defensively aggressive. If your dog has ever been aggressive in a situation like this, call right away to get a private session with an experienced trainer or behaviorist.

Try to avoid reaching under the furniture to grab something away from your puppy.

🐾 PRACTICE MAKES PERFECT

DOWN REVISITED

Remember that most puppies learn to sit on cue much faster than they learn to lie down when you ask. Lying down solely to the word "Down" can take many weeks of training, so don't worry if your pup still needs you to lure him to the floor with a treat in your hand. However, this is a good week to start moving your hand to the floor in a sweeping motion without a treat in it. Start the session out with a treat as usual, and lure your puppy down toward the ground. Once that's worked twice in a row, put the treat in the other hand, but use the same hand you've always used to attract pup's nose to move down. This usually works well because the pup has begun to associate lying down with getting a treat, and your "cue hand" still has the scent of food on it.

Once your pup lies down, give him the treat instantly as usual. If you haven't already, work this week on clarifying the movement of your hand into what will become your visual signal when you are standing up. Hold your hand out toward your pup, and sweep it in a downward arc toward the ground. We like to do it with our palm flat and facing the ground, but all that matters is that you and the rest of your family are consistent.

CONSISTENT CUES?

Speaking of consistent, this is a good week to notice if everyone in the household is consistent when they cue the dog. (Your family wins the rare blue ribbon of consistency if you all are using the exact same signals, both visual and spoken!) Spend a few minutes having everyone ask the dog to sit, down, come and stand. Watch to see if the visual signals are the same. Listen to each family member saying the cue words. Is each word spoken with the same change in pitch? Remember it's not so much what you say, but *how* you say it. If one person says "Down" in a descending tone, and another says it in a rising voice, then the dog is hearing two completely different cues. You can even make it a game for the whole family, and create rewards for those who are the most consistent—after all, we all know that dog training is as much about people training as it is about dogs. Otherwise, you'd just have your puppy read this book, right?

Speaking of reading, one way to help your family be consistent is to write down exactly what words you are using for each cue. Include how you say it, and post it in an obvious place. Refer to it often—you might be surprised at how quickly and easily you begin to modify what you say to your dog until it becomes an entirely different cue.

COME REVISITED

Some people reading this book will have puppies who come absolutely every time they call. Don't be jealous if that doesn't describe your puppy—those folks will join the rest of us later when their dog becomes an adolescent. (See Chapter 6) Either way, it's critical to keep up a program of reinforcing come training during these special weeks. The truth is, you'll need to continue working on come for at least a year, and you should never stop making your dog glad he came when called. However, now is a very special time, when it is easier to condition your dog that coming when called is a good thing to do.

Never stop making your dog glad he came when called!

Set a goal of calling your dog to come 20 times a day. That may seem like a lot, but it's really not. You could accomplish this in less than a total of five minutes, although you should never do it all at once. Call your pup to come when you walk into the kitchen to make his dinner and give him a small piece of his dinner before you put it in the bowl. Call him to come when you're walking down the hall and you have a toy in your pocket to throw when he gets to you. (What? You don't ALWAYS have a toy in your pocket? Start giving yourself a piece of chocolate every time you look down and realize you have something in your pocket to use as spontaneous rewards for your dog!) Say his name out in the yard, and then dash away as you call him to come and be ready to give him that extra tasty treat you were smart enough to bring out with you.

NO JUMPING UP: PHASE TWO

Take advantage of visitors by asking them to have your pup to sit as they enter the house. You should be ready with treats in your hand, so that you can pop the morsel in her mouth the instant she sits down (even if only for a moment). The visitor asks for the sit (both visual and verbal cues would be best here), but you should be the one giving the treats. You'll be much better than your guests are at giving the treats immediately after your puppy sits down.

If your puppy seems too excited by the prospect of greeting someone to remember how to sit on cue, help her out by using food a few times until she understands that sitting is the magic key that gets people to notice and greet her. To help her sit when company comes, put a treat near her nose to get her attention, then draw it quickly behind your back, now repeat your verbal cue to sit, followed by the visual cue if needed. When she does sit, be sure to praise instantly and then give give her that treat you had hidden. She's earned it.

Of course, you should be prepared to ask for a sit every time she greets you too, including when you enter a room, the house or let your pup out of her crate when you come home. Your goal here is simple—to teach her that good things will happen if she sits every times she greets a person.

Don't listen to advice that suggests you step on your dog's back paws or knee her in the chest when she jumps up. Those techniques can scare your dog and can cause injuries (to your dog and to you too—we know someone who slipped and got a concussion doing this). Besides, do you really want to teach your dog that greeting people is dangerous?

WALKING BY YOUR SIDE: NEXT STEPS

Last week you reinforced your puppy for paying more attention to you than anything else outside, treating him every time he noticed you walking away and moving to catch up to you. If necessary, you smooched, clapped or clicked your tongue to encourage him to follow you when you moved away. Ideally, you gave that a try at least once a day, and your pup has now learned that it's fun to follow you around.

This week, try something a little different. Go outside with your pup and a pouch of treats, but this time, try staying quiet and letting your dog follow you of his own accord. Go ahead and show him the treats, but walk away without saying a word, and give him a treat if he notices you leaving his side and catches up to you. Try this off leash if you can, so that there is nothing between you and your puppy. If you have no fenced area, then either let him drag a long line or lightly hold the leash in your hand, trying to avoid it pulling on him as you move away.

Try striding around your pup in a big circle or zig-zagging to the left and right. Your goal here is to walk as if you're on a mission, purposely moving through space without trying to lure your puppy to follow. Watch him out of the corner of your eye, and the instant he approaches within a foot or so, stop walking and give him lots of praise and several wonderful treats. Now try walking away again, watching for the next time he moves toward you. As soon as it feels like he's "caught up," treat him again, and then resume walking. The idea is to teach him to initiate staying with you *on his own*. This self-initiated learning is powerful stuff, and can have a profound effect on how pleasant it is to walk with him when he's grown up.

Guard against expecting a lovely heel from your pup at this phase, and avoid trying to force him to walk quietly by your side on his own. Remember what we said earlier: heeling for dogs is like calculus for people, so work right now on his basic math skills so that he has a solid foundation for more advanced work later on.

SUMMARY

• The way you play with your dog can help you raise a happy, polite dog, or create behavioral problems later in life. Use play to teach obedience, to provide mental and physical exercise, and to help your dog learn emotional control.

• Teach "Drop It" as the flip side of "Take It," so that your dog will eventually drop anything she's picked up at a quiet word from you, rather than running away or growling at you when she has something she shouldn't.

• Fetch is a great game for people and dogs alike—just remember that dogs would rather play keep away. Do everything you can to encourage her to retrieve the toy, and avoid chasing after her when she has the toy in her mouth. Keep your expectations realistic; don't expect a young dog to retrieve endlessly like an adult dog. Stop when she still wants more, and begin the game again later in the day.

• Teach tricks like "Belly Up" and "Find It" to give your dog mental as well as physical exercise.

• Respond to the stealing of objects by distracting her away from the "treasure" if you can. Avoid chasing after her and turning it into a game or a perceived attack. "Puppy proof" the house by keeping tempting objects out of her reach, and encourage her to play with her own toys whenever you can.

• Practice sit, down and stand a little bit every day, incorporating them into daily life instead of just during "training sessions." Ask for her to perform with less luring and in gradually increasing levels of distraction. Continue reinforcing her for responding to her name, and be sure you aren't using her name in ways that will teach her to ignore it!

• Have friends help you teach her not to jump up by always asking for a sit when they greet her, and eventually working with you until she'll sit on her own when someone enters.

• Continue working toward having a dog who is a joy to take on leash walks, by going outside with her and a pouch of treats, and reinforcing her for catching up to you as you walk around her. At this stage, don't encourage with claps or smooches or by calling her name—let her initiate the behavior, and teach her that if she decides to follow you she'll be really, really glad she did.

5

RAISING HAPPY, CONFIDENT PUPPIES

 SPECIAL TOPICS

HELPING YOUR PUPPY CONQUER HIS FEARS

Almost all trainers and behaviorists agree that the most common cause of serious behavioral problems in dogs is fear. Fear is a primal emotion that enables animals to protect themselves, but it doesn't always serve our dogs in every context. Fear can turn into aggression later on in life, and how you deal with it now can have a significant effect on your dog's behavior when he is mature. Let's look at some examples of common fears and how they could be made better—or worse—depending on how they are handled.

A PUPPY'S FIRST VET VISIT, VERSION ONE

When Cassidy went for his first visit to the vet, he got poked, jabbed, prodded and held down forcibly while they clipped his nails, wormed him and vaccinated him. During the appointment he whined and squirmed, and was wide-eyed with fright. His new owner tried to make him feel better by petting and soothing him while he whined, but it didn't seem to help.

This experience will probably make Cassidy wary of his next visit to the vet's office. He may get worse with each appointment, until he becomes an adult dog who is difficult to manage at the clinic.

VERSION TWO

Cassidy's owners scheduled an appointment when the clinic wasn't busy (not on a Monday morning!), so that the staff could take a few extra minutes with him. After he got a chance to sniff around in the lobby, the veterinary technician and veterinarian spent a few minutes greeting him, petting him, and giving him a few treats.

Only the absolute necessities were scheduled for the first visit, making it as pain free and pleasant as possible. Cassidy got several treats while he was up on the table (just for being on the table) and got treats while getting his vaccinations. The nail trim was NOT included in the exam— first impressions can last forever, and the nail trim could wait. Whenever feasible, the ideal first trip to the vet clinic involves no procedures at all—just lots of attention and treats. You want your pup to leave thinking some canine version of "Oh Boy! That was fun! Can we go back?"

Here's another common situation in which a puppy's fears could be either alleviated or heightened:

THE MONSTER IN THE CLOSET

Jake is a puppy with a problem. Every once in a while his owners open the closet at the end of the hall, the one where the monster lives, and let it out to terrorize him. Although the family thinks Jake's attacks on the noisy creature (the one they call a "vacuum") are funny, Jake is serious. The noisy, growly, monster machine is horrifically scary to him, and he thinks he has to "get it before it gets him." The family thinks it's even funnier when they point the monster right at him and have it chase him! He runs to hide in the other room while they have a good laugh about how silly he looks scrambling on the slippery floors.

One day they decide Jake is getting too old for this so they take him by the collar and force him over to the monster machine. Jake is so frightened that he snaps at the monster and then at his owner's hands in a panicked attempt to get away to safety. His owners yell "NO! BAD DOG" and swat him when he does. Eventually they start putting Jake in the yard whenever they vacuum, where he barks and spins when he sees the machine through the window.

This may sound extreme, but trainers and vets hear stories like this all the time. Many owners don't realize how frightened dogs can become, or that "aggressive" behavior is often motivated by fear. Whether it's motivated by fear or something else, growling and biting is dangerous for people and for dogs, so we want to avoid eliciting it from our dogs. Besides, who wants their dog to learn what Jake learned? He learned that vacuum cleaners actually *are* dangerous, just as he feared, and to become frightened and aroused when he sees or hears one. Eventually he might generalize that fear to motorcycles and lawn mowers. He also learned that he can't trust his owners. Not only will they not protect him, they might join the attack and enjoy scaring him. Worst of all, he learned that snapping at frightening things, including people, is an effective way to get away from them. He'll probably try that strategy again sometime, and become labeled as an "aggressive" dog—although he is just trying to protect himself.

These stories illustrate how fears can lead to serious behavioral problems down the road. To avoid a puppy's fears turning into a serious problem, keep the following in mind:

• Learn the signs of fear: puppies who back up, lean away, run away, growl, go stiff, yawn when they're not sleepy, get big, round eyes and/ or flick their tongues in and out are often fearful. Nervous puppies often won't take treats, even ones that they usually love, and aren't interested in playing their favorite games.

• Make a list or mental note of what seems to scare your pup. Shy puppies are often more afraid of men than women, tall people versus short people, and people wearing hats or big jackets.

• Expose your pup to what scares him in a controlled, thoughtful way. If he's afraid of big guys, ask men to stop five feet away and toss treats or toys. Ask them to not lean down and loom over the puppy, and avoid having the puppy picked up abruptly by someone who scares him.

• Link a low-intensity version of what scares your dog with a "good thing," something that makes him happy. Choose the good thing from

Many people don't realize how frightened dogs can become, and that "aggressive" behavior is often motivated by fear.

anything he adores, from food to a great game of tug, and link it with a dampened down version of what scares him. For example, have a stranger stop five feet away and toss treats as he approaches, so that your pup learns to associate the approach of an unfamiliar person with something he loves. If he's afraid of the dishwasher, have someone turn it on while you and the pup are in another room. If he learns that the noise in the kitchen means he gets to play tug, he'll learn to love the sound, just as you learned to love the buzzer in school that meant you could run out to play.

• Don't "flood" your dog with something he's afraid of in hopes he'll get used to it. Often that just makes him worse. Avoid taking a shy puppy to a crowded farmer's market, or taking a dog who is afraid of other dogs into a noisy training class and letting all the other dogs overwhelm him.

If they had followed these suggestions, Jake's family could have helped their pup become comfortable around the vacuum cleaner. They could have played fetch *before* the vacuum was brought out and then continue to play fetch while the vacuum sits quietly in the same room. Next, they could have had someone else turn on the vacuum, in another room, for *just a second*, while they play some more. As Jake came to accept these brief moments of noise in the middle of his playtime, the vacuum could have been turned on for slightly longer periods while they continued to play. Step-by-step the family could have increased the duration of the time the vacuum was on, and have moved it slightly closer to where Jake was playing (or getting treats if that works better). If this progression is followed, Jake eventually will be able to be in the same room with the vacuum running and not be bothered by it.

This process needs to be done at whatever pace Jake's comfort level dictates. If he gets too nervous to play (or take a treat) then they need to back off again and build up more slowly. It may take a few days, or many weeks, but it's well worth the effort. (For more detailed information about this process, see *The Cautious Canine*).

CHILDREN AND PUPPIES

To many of us, the thought of kids and dogs calls up images of children and puppies running joyfully together through fields of daisies. However, ask someone in the business of training and behavior, and they'll tell you that they often associate the mix of kids and dogs with tears and trouble. The fact is, as much as we all want them to get along, children and dogs can get themselves into trouble. As adults, it's our job to keep them out of it. Here's a checklist of ways to ensure that your home is full of Kodak moments, instead of tears and teeth:

• Children and puppies should not be together unsupervised. Period. Kids and young dogs don't know how easily they can hurt or scare one another, and it is your job to monitor their interactions to protect them. Think of it this way: *if you don't protect your puppy from children, you'll be forcing your puppy to protect himself (and vice versa).*

• Adults need to learn the signs of canine discomfort before a dog becomes so stressed that she lashes out. You need to intervene long before a dog starts growling or snapping. See Recommended Reading at the end of the book for in-depth descriptions of stress in our dogs, but in brief: look for a dog who closes her mouth and turns her head away, goes stiff and stops moving, flicks her tongue out straight forward (often a sign of stress or concern), yawns when she's been awake for awhile or attempts to get away.

• That said, keep in mind that puppies will tolerate a lot of things that they find aversive. But just like people, they will become less tolerant as they mature. Don't be lulled by the fact that your five-month old puppy tolerates certain types of interactions—it doesn't mean that she always will.

• Teach children the right way to approach and pet your puppy. Most everyone tells kids to be kind and gentle, but we all need to show them what that means. "Don't smash the puppy on the top of the head with a hammer" is a good start, but we also need to teach children to pet dogs on their chests and cheeks rather than pat-slapping them on the

Teach children the right way to approach and pet your puppy top of their head. Be especially careful of hugs—children are hard-wired to express affection through hugging, but dogs often perceive hugs as rude threats and can be extremely uncomfortable when receiving them.

• Avoid letting puppies be picked up in ways that frighten them. Puppies are often afraid when they are lifted up from terra firma, and why wouldn't they be? They understand the danger of falling by the time they are three weeks old. Children often overestimate their ability to hold onto a squiggly puppy, putting puppies at risk of falling. Imagine being dangled by a giant who had a tentative hold on you while you were 20 feet up in the air. What fun! It's fine to pick up your pup, but make sure that she feels safe and secure when you do so.

• Involve children in the training of your pup as soon as they are able, but don't do this without monitoring the process. Children tend to go to extremes with their commands, almost universally. They repeat commands endlessly when the puppy responds correctly and is already sitting ("Sit. Sit. Sit. Sit. Sit. Sit."), and then repeat commands endlessly when the puppy doesn't respond and is doing something else. ("Sit. Sit. Sit. Sit. Sit. Sit.") Enough said.

Teach children to pet dogs on the side of the dogs' head only if the dog approaches first.

• Teach children to play appropriately with your pup. Emphasize games that direct the puppy away from the child's face and hands. Games like "Find It" or "Where's Mom?" are great, as are tricks like "Sit Pretty." You might want to have each child teach a special trick to the dog. (But do remember, no dog wants to roll over 57 times in one day!). Fetch games are great once the dog has been taught (by you) to bring the toy back. Avoid unsupervised chase games in which the puppy chases the kids (or worse, the kids chase the puppy). Running, giggling, screaming kids are just too much for most puppies, causing the pup to behave inappropriately with the kids. (Supervised "come" games in which the child stops as the puppy approaches are fine as long as the pup isn't using his mouth when he catches up.)

• Don't encourage rowdy behavior in the house from your pup, any more than you would encourage your children to play softball near the family's heirloom china. If a pup spends an excessive amount of time running around and barking in the house now, he will be rowdy in the house as an adult.

• All dogs need times to be left alone, and kids must be taught that sometimes one should "let sleeping dogs lie."

• Even if you follow all the suggestions above to the letter, some dogs will never be comfortable around children. We hope you don't find yourself in this situation, but if you do, please reach out for help—find a positive-based trainer or behaviorist who can evaluate the situation and help you resolve the problem, keeping the welfare of you, your children and your dog uppermost in their mind.

One last comment about children and dogs who are not part of the family: It's important to teach your own children never to approach strange dogs without permission from you *and* the dog's owner. Not all dogs will be as friendly as your pup. Even friendly dogs may get frightened by unfamiliar children who run up and hug them. Teach your child to stop three to four feet away from a dog, hold out their hand and ask the dog to come to them. If the dog doesn't approach on its own, then no one (including you) should reach out and try to pet it. Teach visiting children to behave the same way around your own dog, and always supervise children when they are interacting with your puppy.

 NEW EXERCISES

THE "PUPPY PAUSE"

Asking a puppy to sit still without getting up while distracted is like asking a toddler to sit quietly while all of his friends are running around in the same room. However, teaching a solid stay is actually not hard, *if* you have realistic expectations and approach it as a game that your puppy can't lose. Young dogs need time and maturity to develop the

> *Build the foundation of stay by teaching "Puppy Pauses" first.*

emotional control needed to stay in place when distracted, but you can start now and create the foundation of a solid stay that will eventually do you and your dog proud. To get there, start with "Puppy Pauses," by reinforcing your dog if he holds the sitting position for a second or two.

Begin by asking your pup to sit in an area with few distractions. Immediately, give him a treat for sitting, and then *another* treat while he's still sitting down. As long as he continues to stay seated, keep giving him treats, one right after the other. As you do, use an under-handed motion to move the morsels all the way to his mouth. Don't make him get up to reach for the treat—that's defeating the purpose! Continue to give him treats for three or four seconds while he's is planted on the ground. The instant he gets up on his own, withdraw the treats and walk away. Start again a minute later, and he'll soon learn that this "extended sit" keeps the treats coming.

Try this on a daily basis. It won't take much time, just a few seconds several times a day can condition your dog to enjoy sitting still. Remember, for this week, guard against the ever-so-human desire to say something (like "Stay"). Right now you are building the foundation, not painting the house! Next week's exercises will introduce the second step toward a reliable stay for the time when your dog is mature enough to handle it.

 PRACTICE MAKES PERFECT

NO JUMPING UP REVISITED

If you've been practicing having your puppy sit when company arrives, try asking visitors to help you take her manners to the next level. Begin with your usual routine in which a visitor asks for a sit, and you praise and treat. Repeat that right away, one more time. Repeat again, but this time have the visitor approach, stand still and remain silent for a few seconds. This will give your pup a chance to initiate the sit himself.

That's the goal—to have a dog who automatically sits when visitors come to call.

Pay extra careful attention when you try this. If your pup sits, praise quietly (don't get him hyped up and jumping in response to your reinforcement), and give him a "jackpot" of treats—ten treats in a row! You want him to be stunned at your generosity, and wondering what on earth he did to deserve all that food! Don't worry if he doesn't sit on his own the first time you give him the opportunity. Just go back to asking him to sit, and try a bit later for him to initiate it himself. Be patient, he's just a kid after all, and it takes emotional maturity and impulse control for young dogs to pull this off.

He will learn fastest if you have a friend repeat this routine several times in one visit. Ideally, have a "puppy party" in which lots of friends come over, enter the house one at a time, and give your pup a chance to sit on his own. Every time he does, he gets lots of treats, until he can't wait to do it again the next time the doorbell rings.

TAKE IT/DROP IT: PHASE 2

Once your pup will readily drop a toy when you say "Drop It" and give her a treat, it's time to expand her repertoire so that you can begin to use the cue when you need it. Begin this next phase by playing the game as you have previously. Encourage her to take a toy as you say "Take It." Play tug for a few seconds, then say "Drop It" and move a treat toward her mouth. Hopefully, at this stage, she dropped the toy after you said "Drop It" but before the food arrived at her mouth. Give her lots of praise and the treat, to remind her how much fun it is to open her mouth when she hears you say "Drop It."

After a few repetitions, give her the toy again (if she'll take it; if not, wait a minute without giving her any food and try again) but this time, *withdraw your hold on the toy* and let her play with it by herself. After a few seconds, say "Drop It" and if she does, immediately have a party and give her a couple of treats. The difference here may seem small, but it's a big one to her. Possession is the law in canine society, and

> *"Jackpots" are great ways to reinforce an especially good response.*

once you dropped your grip on the toy, it became "hers." Asking her to drop it now is very different than asking her to drop it when you still had a hold of it. You're not going to be holding on to the other side of some stinky food wrapper that she finds in the gutter once you're ready to use this cue, so don't skip this step in her training!

As you progress over a period of months, you can replace the food treat with another toy, or pick up the toy you started with and play some more. As she matures, ask her to drop an object in increasingly challenging situations—when you are farther away, when she has something she considers to be a treasure and when you don't have a toy or a treat handy. Be mindful of the difficulty level here, and only "push the envelope" one step at a time. Asking her to drop a moderately interesting toy when you're standing beside her with treats is a far cry from asking her to drop a piece of food that she found on the sidewalk. If you skip the intermediate steps, then six months down the road you will be less successful when you ask her to drop the disgusting thing that she just found in the street.

WALKING BY YOUR SIDE: MAKING PROGRESS

Continue giving your pup treats when he catches up to you and is in heel position, facing the same way as you, but now try it with him attached to the leash (if you haven't yet). It's amazing how every little change can make a difference; so start practicing as if you were going on a neighborhood walk. Keep watch on him out of the corner of your eye, so that you can be ready to reinforce him as soon as he moves to your side. Use your treat if need be to lure him into the position you want. If he ignores you, stop and stand still, but be ready to praise and treat the second he looks in your direction. Inevitably, there will be times that he is lost in his nose, sniffing something compelling in the grass and completely ignoring you. If this goes on too long, walk a few feet away, clapping or smooching to get his attention. Show him a treat, but don't give it to him, just remind him of the benefits of paying attention. Move off a few feet again, then praise and treat generously when and if he follows you and catches up of his own accord.

Keep these sessions short, using the body harness or other tools when you go on longer neighborhood walks. Remember that heeling is hard work (try it yourself beside a friend, it's harder than it looks, even for a species that walks side-by-side naturally!). Be especially generous with treats for this exercise—professional trainers will tell you that most people use too few treats when teaching their dogs to walk politely on leash. Practice this for short periods several times a day when you can; even a few seconds two or three times a day can have an impact later in life. Avoid using any words as a cue yet—we'll add a cue on next week if things are going well.

SUMMARY

• Fear can cause behavioral problems in adult dogs, so act now to teach your dog that visitors, vacuum cleaners and vets aren't anything to be afraid of. Link something your pup loves with a damped down version of something that might scare him. Don't force interactions and overwhelm him with too much, too soon.

• Supervise children and dogs, teaching each of them how to be polite to each other. Learn the subtle signs of discomfort in your pup so that you can avoid interactions that make him nervous. Don't hesitate to intervene, quietly and politely, if either child or dog begins to harass their playmate.

• Teach your dog "Puppy Pauses" by asking for a sit, and then giving him treats as long as he stays in a seated position for a few seconds. If he gets up, dramatically remove the treats and walk away yourself. At this point you are just building the foundation, so don't say "Stay" yet, just ask for a sit and treat as he remains seated.

• Begin asking your dog to "Drop It" when you no longer have a hold of the object yourself. Give lots of reinforcement for correct responses, and gradually build on them, by asking him to drop things when 1) you are farther away, 2) he has a higher value object in his mouth or 3) you are plumb out of treats or toys. Do this step-by-step, only upping the difficulty level one factor at a time, and give lots and lots of reinforcement for correct responses in challenging situations.

• Continue working on polite leash manners by adding the leash into the "Walking by your Side" exercise. Generously treat him every time he catches up to you, remembering how hard this is for dogs, especially young ones. Don't use the cue "Heel" yet, and if your dog doesn't follow you when you walk away a few feet and wait for him to catch up, go back to him and show him a treat. Don't give it to him, just remind him what he's missing, and try again.

6

ADOLESCENCE AND OTHER QUANDARIES

★ SPECIAL TOPICS

AH ADOLESCENCE!

Adolescence is a time of change for your pup just as it is for human teenagers, and it isn't always easy on the rest of us. Young dogs begin to get more independent, and they begin testing the boundaries, not to mention your patience. Somewhere between five to seven months, your previously docile puppy may become impossible one day and go back to being an angel the next. Just when you are feeling proud of how much you and your dog have progressed, your training goes backward rather than forward.

The good news is that this won't last forever if we handle it correctly. All we need to do is to calmly and quietly carry through on our cues—if we asked for a sit, then we need to be sure our puppy sits before moving on to something else. It takes patience (insert laughing here due to profound understatement), because patience and a calm, quiet attitude work wonders. What is most important is that if you ask your dog to do something, you ensure that he does it. There's no need to shout or to use harsh corrections—as a matter of fact they should be avoided. Instead, be benevolently persistent. Accept that the dog who had mastered sitting on cue will look at you one day as if he'd never heard the word before. It's fine for you to back up in your training a bit and help him out—repeat visual signals or use food as a lure, gently attach the leash, but in any case, see to it that if you asked him to come, he came. If you asked for a sit, don't allow him to move on to something else without sitting first. Don't worry if it takes some time to get it done—there's no hurry here, as long as it gets done in the end. During doggy adolescence, it is especially important to impress upon your pup that it's in his best interest to do what you ask. No matter how long it took to get what you wanted, don't move on until it happens.

TAKE A TIP FROM US Here's a tip from professional trainers that will make your life much easier: Only give cues when you are ready and able to carry through with them, otherwise he'll learn to ignore you. For example, don't let him off leash at the park with a gang of puppy hooligans and then call him to come when you know he won't listen. Instead, either don't let it happen in the first place, or use it as a "teachable moment." Rather than calling him to come from a distance, go to him and get his attention with a treat. (This may involve all owners working together at the same time.) Lure him a few steps away from his buddies and THEN call him to come to you. Granted it'll be a recall of only three or four feet, but he'll have learned that it's fun to come when called—especially if you then let him go off and play some more.

Make a mental note of the situations in which you're having trouble and work on a step-by-step training progression to help him respond when he is distracted. Never forget that you are competing for his attention with the environment—with other dogs, great smells, or interesting animals to chase. Having a dog who listens and responds to you no matter what isn't about dominance at all, it's about winning the competition for his attention.

GENERALIZE THE CUES Guard against the beginner's tendency to get into a routine and only ask for certain responses in specific contexts. Just about everybody's dog will sit when asked in the kitchen while the owner is holding up the dinner bowl, but that doesn't automatically transfer to the vet clinic or to someone coming to the door. Go out of your way to mix it up: play "Puppy Pauses" during a commercial break while you're watching television, call her to come when you're walking down the hall and reinforce her by speeding up yourself as she moves in your direction. Ask for a down before you throw a toy. The trick is to vary the jobs and rewards so that she never knows what she'll be asked to do next. Besides keeping your adolescent busy, you'll be reminding her to pay attention.

EXERCISE EXERCISE EXERCISE! Give your pup as much exercise as your veterinarian will allow. Older puppies need less sleep than when they were younger, and need an increasing amount of physical and mental exercise. This is a great time to work on teaching tricks and new exercises—learning something new uses up energy and is a great way to tire out your dog. Take your dog to a place where it is safe for him to be off leash, but only if you have a bag of tasty treats with you. Call "Come!" several times on the walk, before your pup gets too far away. When he turns to look, praise him and run like heck the other way to let him enjoy a chase game. Give him the snack when he catches up.

Guard against one problem that can occur when exercising your pup: don't hype your dog up right before it's time for him to settle down. Just like children, getting wild-eyed and excited before bedtime is not the best way to nod off to dream land. Try giving your pup mental exercise, as described in Chapter 4 and the booklet *Play Together, Stay Together*, to tire your dog out before it's time to go to sleep.

BARKING AT VISITORS

Even bold, friendly puppies can go through a period in their lives when they become frightened by things that had no effect on them when they were younger. Experts agree that there is a "fear period" experienced by many dogs around early adolescence, usually around six to nine months. This is often the age that you may first see a puppy back away from a visitor, perhaps remaining silent but stiff, or begin to bark at strangers.

> *As your dog matures, vary the exercises and reinforcements so that she learns to respond any time, anywhere.*

This is a sign that your puppy is becoming afraid of unfamiliar people, and his fear of strangers can turn into aggression when he grows up. If you see your puppy begin to act fearfully, don't panic, but take steps immediately to condition your dog to associate strangers with good things. As explained in Chapter 5, if you see signs of fear or discomfort in your pup, have visitors toss treats while still five feet away. Don't force an interaction, and avoid passing a puppy around like a doll when visitors come over—it's fun for us but not for the pup![6]

> *If your young dog shows even subtle signs of shyness around strangers, it's important to turn that around as soon as you can.*

If your young dog shows even subtle signs of shyness around strangers, it's important to turn that around as soon as you can. Most dogs, including many that we have owned, can come out of this period as reliable, people-loving dogs. However, to prevent problems in the future, you do need to take action. Teach your pup that the approach of strangers means wonderful things are about to happen. Visitors might toss a ball as they approach or enter the yard throwing tasty treats. At our houses, deliverymen are asked to throw balls for our dogs if they have an extra 5 seconds. Usually this conditioning procedure only needs to last four or five months, but the wise owner of a slightly fearful dog never hesitates to take the opportunity to link the approach of a visitor with something good.

OTHER DOGS HAVE STARTED GROWLING AT MY PUP

Polite adult canines grant young dogs a "puppy license," just as we'd allow a young child to do things we'd never put up with once they are older. Imagine the difference in reaction between a three-year old boy running up to a police officer and trying to play with his gun, versus an eighteen-year old doing it! Puppy licenses expire around early adolescence, and older dogs begin to enforce the rules of polite canine society with body slams, growls and tooth displays. This can look frightening, but remember that it is appropriate for dogs to use these displays when communicating.[7]

6 Word to the wise: Forced interactions are a common mistake made by dog owners. Trainers around the country are tearing their hair out as you read this at the number of dogs who have been made MORE afraid of visitors by being forced into scary encounters with strangers.

7 A note to those with un-neutered males over six months of age: You may see even stronger reactions from other dogs, given that the testosterone levels in adolescent male dogs are more than ten times higher

However, not all reactions to your pup are appropriate, so pay careful attention to the other dog's behavior. Responses to your pup will vary; much as one person might react differently than another if you accidentally stepped on their toes. One person might ignore it, another might give an understanding smile, while yet another might get downright nasty. For your pup's sake, you want to look for dogs who give appropriate, inhibited responses. If your pup dashes up to a mature dog and dances on his head, a dog is well within his rights to respond with a quick growl or a show of the teeth. If, however, the growl leads to slamming your pup to the ground and standing over him while continuing to growl, you'd be wise to intervene. Warnings are one thing, attacks are another.

It can take some experience to know what is appropriate and what is not in dog-dog interactions, and this is one of the great benefits of working with a trainer in a well-managed puppy class. Good instructors will go out of their way to highlight appropriate versus inappropriate interactions and illustrate how to intervene when necessary.

YOUR BEHAVIOR HAS AN INFLUENCE How you behave when your dog is greeting or playing with others is also important.

Here are some tips:
• Try to keep the leashes loose when you and your pup meet unfamiliar dogs. Tension on the leash can create tension in your dog.

• Avoid standing in a circle around greeting dogs and staring at them with baited breath. If you go stiff and hold your breath, you are mimicking a dog's posture when warning of an impending attack. Go out of your way to stay loose and relaxed. Breathe! If you are truly nervous about your dog greeting another dog, then avoid it by moving away or distracting the dogs onto something else.

• Redirect any tension between two greeting dogs by engaging them in another activity. For example, you could say in a cheerful voice "OK, let's go for a walk!" and stride purposefully away.

than when they are adults. The presence of all those hormones can have a big impact on how other dogs react to your adolescent male, as well as affecting his behavior toward them.

• Don't make a fuss if another dog scares your pup. Try to be calm and matter-of-fact, so that she will feel confident and safe because of your example. Later, set up play dates with extra polite dogs, especially ones (if you can) that look like the dog that scared her. If a black Lab frightened her, find some friendly black Labs for her to play with, so she doesn't learn to fear big black dogs in general.

• An occasional spat[8], is a normal part of being an adolescent pup, but if it happens often or is severe, contact a professional for help in figuring out why, and to get advice on how to handle it.

MY PUPPY URINATES DURING GREETINGS

This is a relatively normal canine behavior called *submissive urination* and was never a problem until we started bringing dogs into our homes. Who cares if they urinate in the dirt? But most of us love sharing our houses with dogs, and would rather skip cleaning up urine from the carpet. The good news is that most pups will outgrow submissive urination within a few months, but there are things you can do to speed up the process.

• First, never scold your puppy for urinating during greetings, it will just make the problem worse. This is not something he consciously decided to do, and scolding will just make him feel more insecure and submissive. He'll be even worse the next time you approach, so hold your tongue! (Alternatively, take a tip from us and speak sweetly, but using words that match your feelings: "Oh Rover!" (You say with kindness and love in your voice.) "I am SO thrilled that I have to clean this up again. What was I thinking when I brought you home? Maybe I should return you for a refund?" (She said, with a happy lilt in her voice.)

• If you can, try to greet your pup on a vinyl floor or outside, so that it isn't a problem to clean it up. This might mean opening the crate door and running outside with your pup before you say hello, but that's okay. (And say "Come" as you turn away and run to the door!)

8 For example, an interaction including a few growls, and a tooth display, but with no biting or injury of any kind.

• Don't lean over your pup as you greet him. Instead kneel down, with your weight leaning slightly back away from him and let him come to you. The primary triggers of submissive urination are rapid approaches (the taller the person the more intimidating) and looming over the head and body of the puppy.

• Keep your good-byes and homecomings low key. Let your pup think that having you come and go is no big deal.

• Get in the habit of coming into the house flinging food to one side or the other, while you walk straight ahead, ignoring the puppy. This seems to help switch the pup out of greeting mode and directs their attention elsewhere. Put a bag or can of treats outside your door, and ask visitors to toss them *away from the dog* as they enter. Just a week of this has cured some dogs who emptied their bladders whenever a stranger walked in the door.

• Ask: Is anyone yelling at your pup, or being harsh with him? A pup that urinates submissively needs a lot of confidence building, and will be extra sensitive to loud or harsh corrections. This is yet another reason to focus on using positive reinforcement.

WHAT ABOUT MY OTHER DOGS?

It's one thing to raise a puppy by himself, but it's another to integrate her into a home with other dogs. Here are some things to keep in mind if you have a multi-dog household:

ONE AT A TIME Spend some time working separately with each dog, especially the new one. You are going to be the odd one out if your new pup is always playing with members of her own species. After all, dogs speak the same language, and even if you "speak dog," you do it with a strong accent! If you want your new puppy to bond to you, to listen to you and to love being with you, then she needs individualized attention. Use play between the two of you to teach her that it's fun to listen, and that you are the best game in town.

> *All dogs should learn that they get what they want by being patient and polite, not by throwing their weight around.*

ALPHA SCHMALPHA Don't try to set up one dog or another as "alpha" over the other(s). Your job is to be the benevolent leader, or the parent if you will, who establishes the boundaries and who is a role model for acceptable behavior. All dogs should learn that they get what they want by being patient and polite, not by throwing their weight around. Teach all the dogs to wait at doors until released (one at a time), defer to others who are being petted and to do "Group down-stays." Teaching all of that is beyond the scope of a puppy book, so see the booklet, *Feeling Outnumbered?* for details on how to accomplish this, or talk to your class instructor. For now, remember your job is to teach your dog that the patient and polite shall inherit the earth.

GAMES HAVE RULES TOO It's absolutely fine to let your puppy play with older dogs in the house if they seem to be getting along well. As described above, dogs often play by using their teeth, by mock biting and growling . . . basically being dogs! Don't be too concerned about the noises they make or the teeth you see unless one of them seems frightened, or one gets carried away and seems overly aroused. If that happens, then quietly step in and distract him. Don't yell or correct— you'll just add to the tension.

Until your pup is mature, it's a good idea not to leave him loose in the house with the other dogs if you are going to be gone for any length of time. Besides housetraining and chewing issues, it's a good idea not to let your pup play with the other dogs for hours on end with no "playground monitor." Besides, if your pup spends all of her time playing with your other dog(s), where do you come in?

YOU'RE THE REFEREE It's your job to monitor what's going on between the dogs. If an old, or very submissive dog looks as though he is being harassed by the puppy, gently stop the pup and either put her in her crate or redirect her to something else. Your older dog deserves some peace and quiet. Puppies can be tiring (did you notice?) and if you don't protect your older dog from her, then he'll be forced to protect himself. Not having access to lawyers or the ability to post nasty blogs on Facebook, he'll have no recourse but to use his teeth.

You may need to step in if an adult dog is putting up with all kinds of abuse from the newcomer. Intervene and redirect the puppy if she is being rude, so that she doesn't learn to be a bully. A patient dog is a blessing, but you don't want your pup to grow up thinking she can do anything to any dog and get away with it. If your older dog is endlessly forgiving, be sure that your pup does play with dogs who set limits.

On the other hand, if your older dog or dogs are being rude or truly aggressive to your pup, you'd be wise to call in an experienced trainer or behaviorist. It can be tricky to decide what is appropriate and what is not, and this is when a skilled eye can be of great help. Don't wait too long to get help, lest your young pup learn early on that other dogs are dangerous.

HOME ALONE

We all have to leave the house sometimes, whether it's to go to work or to deposit our lottery winnings into the bank. Having a dog who is comfortable and reliable in the house is a gift beyond measure—ask anyone who *doesn't* have it! Problems with dogs left home alone are a frequent cause of appointments with behaviorists and surrenders at shelters, so don't take this part of puppy raising lightly. You may previously have had a dog who had no problems when left alone, but take our word for it, all dogs are different. It's worth going out of your way to prevent having a dog who makes your arrival home into an adventure. Here are some tips to ensure that your homecoming is filled with happy, body wagging greetings instead of a house full of chewed up furniture and wet, smelly carpets.

IN THE CRATE OR SMALL ROOM? Give your dog extra chances to potty before you go. Do not assume he has urinated or defecated just because he was outside. (Would you assume a one-year old child would use the toilet because there is one in the house?) Go out with him right before you leave, use your cue and reinforce with a food treat if he goes.

Provide lots of exercise before you leave, but avoid hyping your pup up just minutes before you go. Try, if you can, to end the exercise session a good 30 minutes before you leave, so that your pup can settle down once he goes into the crate.

Put a safe toy that is stuffed with food into the crate or sleeping area just as you are leaving. You want your pup to run into this space with happy anticipation when you pick up your keys and put on your jacket. If you condition your dog that wonderful things happen right after you get ready to go, you are well on your way to having a dog who settles down and sleeps while you're gone. Once you've gotten the habit well established (6 to 12 months), you can skip the stuffed toy and occasionally give your dog a small treat once he is in the crate.

Be sure that your dog is not confined to the crate or sleeping area for longer than he can hold his bladder. Young dogs simply can't control their bladders while you're away at work all day long. If you have to be gone all day, arrange for someone to come at lunchtime and let your pup outside to potty. You just can't have it both ways—if the crate or sleeping area is to be a good place, then the time he spends there must be pleasant, not a nightmare of trying to squeeze his furry, little legs together.

OUT OF THE CRATE? Many people think that they can leave a four-month old puppy alone loose in the house because he hasn't had an accident in the house for weeks and must be "housetrained." Au contraire! Young dogs need lots of time to fully establish good house habits, including holding it when they have to potty and only chewing on dog toys instead of the couch. Most trainers and breeders would never think of leaving a dog unattended in the house for any length of time until they are well over a year of age, if not older. Start slowly; try leaving your dog with a food-stuffed toy when you walk to the mailbox, then when you run to the local store and will only be gone ten minutes. If you find trouble when you return, no scolding allowed! Just make a note that your pup isn't ready yet, and take two steps backward in your training progression.

NO BIG DEAL If you want your comings and goings to be accepted by your pup as part of daily life, then make your exits and entrances low key. Your pup can easily learn to behave hysterically around visitors if he gets elaborate, emotional greetings on a routine basis. We're not saying you shouldn't greet him when you come home (who could resist!) but try to give him a relatively quiet hello, and stay low key until the excitement of your entrance dies down. You'd also be wise to avoid leaving with a guilt-laden speech about how badly you feel that you have to leave. Patricia was racked with guilt whenever she left her first Border Collie, Drift, until someone wisely pointed out to her that she was going to work, while her dog was going to lie around and snooze all day. She began saying "Do a good job!" as she left, meaning "Your job is to settle down, chew only on dog toys and avoid going potty in the house. My job is to earn the money I spend on your toys and food, you lucky dog you." It made leaving a lot easier for her, and probably easier for Drift as well.

A SOOTHING ENVIRONMENT The environment can have a significant effect on your dog's behavior when you are gone. Leaving a dog next to a window, for example, might seem soothing to us humans, but it often over stimulates dogs who can see squirrels and other dogs walking by. It's better to leave your dog in a place that is both acoustically and visually quiet, but is not so far out of your normal living area that the dog feels he's been warehoused in an unfamiliar environment.

Putting your dog's crate by a window might be over stimulating and end up causing more harm than good.

You can also leave on a radio station that plays quiet classical or "easy listening" music while you are gone. (Avoid hard rock and talk radio stations, which can be stressful for dogs.) The radio can help to mask outside noises and might make your pup feel less alone. Many dogs are also soothed by the presence of a plug-in pheromone dispenser called D.A.P.® or Comfort Zone. You can't smell it, but your dog's brain perceives it to be the pheromone that is produced by a mother dog when she is nursing her puppies. All you have to do is buy it and plug it in—what could be easier that that?

MY PUPPY GETS CAR SICK

You have our sympathy. We've been there and it's not fun for anyone, especially when the pup gets sick all over the backseat just as you arrive at your destination (a frustratingly common phenomenon). Take heart, because most puppies outgrow carsickness as they mature. The inner ear canal is not fully developed in young dogs, which can cause motion sickness, and its subsequent nausea and vomiting, but the problem resolves as they mature. Nervousness or fear of the car may magnify this effect.

TRIPS TO NOWHERE Help her to overcome her fears by associating the car with wonderful things. Start by playing with her in the car, perhaps with her favorite toy, while the doors are open (engine off, car in the driveway). When she's old enough, teach her to jump in and out of the car as if it were a circus trick. If she's afraid of the car itself, even when the engine is off, start by feeding her treats beside the car while it is turned off and motionless in the driveway. Then feed her inside the car door, then further inside the car, then all the way inside and start the engine running. Gradually allow her to become more comfortable at each level before progressing to the next. We've had great luck with letting a pup watch another dog jump in and out of a parked car. Turn the tables on your pup and don't let her go into the car while the other dog gets lots of treats or ball play for doing so—the Huck Finn approach works on dogs too!

While your pup is young, take short daily trips—only a few hundred yards—while someone feeds her tiny bits of liver. (Go easy on the amount of food. We suspect we don't need to tell you why!) Drive for one block, then get out and take her on a short, fun walk. Drive her a little further each time. Before a longer trip it's usually best not to feed your pup for several hours before leaving. Work on the "treat therapy" at a separate time, using toys instead of food to jolly her up on longer trips.

SAFETY FIRST A dog loose in the car is in a dangerous position, and puts others at risk as well. Any abrupt stop can send the dog flying through the car, injuring themselves or others in the process. Serious accidents can result in a dog who is thrown out of the car, and is then at risk of being struck by another vehicle or running away in terror. Use either crates or a doggy seat belt to keep your dog safe. Covered crates have the advantage of reducing a dog's chance of getting sick in the car. They also make it less likely your pup will begin dashing back and forth from window to window, barking at other cars or dogs on the street. Trust us, you want to prevent this common problem.

I KNOW MY PUP NEEDS EXERCISE, BUT HOW MUCH?

An accurate answer is almost always: "However much exercise your dog is getting—it's probably not enough!" With that said, let's be realistic. Dogs, especially young ones, do indeed need lots of exercise, but it's no good feeling guilty about it. It is wise to prevent behavioral problems by giving your dog plenty of exercise, but there are ways to get your dog's needs met that aren't a burden on you.

First off, start by defining "exercise" broadly. The process of learning tricks and "obedience" exercises is strenuous mental exercise, and can tire out a dog as much as a long walk. Playing fetch is great exercise that doesn't involve much effort on your part. Once your pup is retrieving well (see "Fetch" in Chapter 4), try a tennis racket, or a ball launcher that helps you throw the ball farther while sparing your arm. Set up puppy play dates several times a week and let your dog romp with others— they're more efficient than we are at wearing one another out!

Create routines that make it easy to interact with your dog in a way that gets him moving and thinking. Teach a new trick during a commercial break while watching television. Teach your dog to "Go Find" a hidden toy in another room while you finish making dinner, or do the same in the backyard. Enroll in training classes appropriate to your pup's age and development, and take advantage of the social interaction and mental exercise involved. Find safe places to walk and go on long walks where your dog is free to be off leash, and explore on her own. (Be cautious of dog parks when your dog is young, they can be overwhelming to young pups, and are not safe until your dog has had all of her vaccinations.)

> *Mental exercise is as good for your pup as physical exercise.*

Biking or jogging with you can be a good form of exercise for adult dogs, but can cause problems in puppies whose bones and joints aren't finished developing. A safe age to start repetitive exercise varies by breed, it can be anywhere from 1 to 2 years, or even later. Be sure to check with your veterinarian before doing either of these forms of exercise with your pup. Regardless of your dog's age, avoid frequent running on hard pavement, which is tough on any dog. If you do try bicycling with your dog, be sure to use a safe attachment (like a "Springer") that prevents your dog from pulling you over if she bolts after a squirrel.

Keep in mind that a walk around the block once or twice a day is not enough exercise for most dogs. Of course, very young puppies, eight to ten weeks old, can only do so much, but by the time a dog is four to five months old he is much stronger, and needs a lot more exercise. This exercise requirement usually peaks around eight months to three years of age (sorry, we did indeed say "years"!), so start finding ways to keep your dog busy now. Don't, however, feel duty bound to walk your dog around the neighborhood twice a day, day in and day out. Dogs need physical exercise and mental stimulation, but it's okay to occasionally skip the walk one evening and play in the backyard, or teach a new trick in the living room instead. Teach your dog to potty in your own yard or close to your apartment (a good idea for all of us), clean up after her no matter where you are, and go back inside and play "Find the Stuffed Squirrel!" Routines have their value, but don't get trapped by them. Mix it up a little bit; it'll be good for both of you. Just don't skip the walk and end up not doing anything at all with your dog. Until dogs start watching television and surfing the internet, they are dependent on us for stimulation and exercise.

BARKING: THE GOOD, THE BAD AND THE LOUD

Barking usually begins as a dog matures, although some puppies seem to bark on delivery and others remain silent most of their lives. No matter when it starts, we humans seem to be ambivalent about barking—sometimes we want our dogs to alert us when they see something they think is important; other times we want them to keep quiet about it. Until we breed dogs who can read our minds, this is a bit of a quandary. The best way to prevent barking from becoming a problem (and believe us, it's high on the list of owner irritations) is to have a plan for how to handle it, and to clearly communicate to your pup when and where not to bark.

DANGER! DANGER! ALIENS COMING! The most common motivation for barking is when something or someone out of the family enters the "territory." Some people encourage this because they want a guard dog, but we strongly caution against this. A few alerting barks are great, but the last thing you want is a dog who views visitors as potentially dangerous. Yes, she might stop a burglar, but she is more likely to scare off a neighbor or go after emergency responders when you called 911.

Of course, most of us are not encouraging our dogs to bark when company comes, we are desperately trying to get them to be quiet. A common response is to say something like "Be Quiet!" or, in desperation, "Shut Up!" Of course, to a dog, we are simply joining in the barking—the more we yell, the louder they bark. Thus, Job One when getting a handle on a dog's barking is to put your hand over your mouth and be quiet yourself. (We didn't say this was easy.)

THANK YOU FOR STOPPING BARKING To get control over your pup's barking, regardless of the reason for it, teach her a cue that means "that first bark or two was enough." Use a simple phrase like "Enough" or "Thank You." Start by presenting a stimulus that elicits barking (knocking on the door for example), then taking it away (stop knocking on the door). As the noise stops, go all the way to your dog, say "Thank You," and use a yummy treat to lure her away from the direction she is facing. Once she's stopped barking and taken a few steps away from the door, give her the treat. Of course, she only stopped barking because the reason for it went away, but look what happened here:

- Something caused her to bark.
- You said "Thank You."

> *Avoid yelling "Be Quiet!" when your dog is barking, he'll think you're joining the chorus!*

- She stopped barking.

- She got reinforced with a tasty piece of food.

If she is persistent in her barking, put a smelly, luscious treat *within an inch* of her nose to catch her attention and interrupt her barking. Be sure to say "Thank You!" just before the treat arrives. Don't give her the food yet, use it to lure her away a few feet away from the door, and then praise and give her the treat. Be sure she gets the treat before she starts barking again, otherwise you'll defeat the purpose. Gradually extend the time she is expected to be quiet before she gets the treat. Once she stops barking, redirect her to some other activity to help keep her mind occupied. Over time, begin to ask her to stop barking when the stimulus to bark continues (the knock at the door), but remember that this takes a lot of emotional control on her part and can take a long time to master. Eventually you can drop out the treat, but this is a hard exercise for dogs to master, so be patient. If you find that you've tried the steps above and your ears are still ringing from problematic barking, either have your dog read this section herself, or call in a professional to work through it with you.

YO! YOU! PAY ATTENTION! Another reason that dogs bark is to get your attention. If, in response, you pet her, throw her toy, get up to let her outside or even talk back to her, she is getting your attention. Bingo! Success! Therefore, if she is barking *at you*, do your best to ignore her until she is quiet. Turn your head away or turn your back on her if she is being pushy or demanding. You could even leave the room until she quiets down. As soon as she is quiet, ask her to do something for you (sit or down, for example), then give her the attention she wants.

HEY! HEY! HEY! Dogs left outside by themselves for long periods often develop a barking problem. Perhaps it begins out of nervousness, loneliness, boredom, or a feeling that they were left out on "guard duty." Many dogs appear to become stressed by this perceived responsibility and overreact at every little noise or movement, or perhaps some of them are simply over stimulated. Either can lead to a lot of problematic behaviors as your dog matures. You can avoid this type of barking problem by training her how to be a good girl inside the house, and keeping her inside when you are gone rather than outside in the yard. We've seen hundreds of dogs over the years who may love it outside *with you*, but don't do well if left alone in a backyard all day. Often, they are subject to teasing from neighbor children (a more common problem than you might guess), or over stimulation by chattering chipmunks and passing dogs. If your dog has to be left outside when you are gone, house him in an area where he is protected from teasing and is not over stimulated by the environment.

 ## PRACTICE MAKES PERFECT

TURNING PUPPY PAUSES INTO STAYS

Continue to "prime" your puppy for stay training by asking for a sit, and then giving him treats until he gets up. Remember, at this stage, you're not asking him to stay, you're just conditioning him that it's fun to sit down and keep his behind on the ground for a while. Keep this up for a few days, and then, if it's going well, try the next step:

Ask for a sit, and then, before you hand him his expected treat, add in the cues that you'll use to tell him to stay. Move your hand forward, palm toward your pup like a traffic cop blocking traffic, and say "Stay" in a flat or descending tone. Then freeze for an instant—*less than a second*—maintaining eye contact with your pup. Count "one one-thousand," and then move a treat all the way to the puppy's mouth and let him eat it.

Give him one or two more treats, and then release him by saying "Free" or "Okay." Don't forget the release word (a very common mistake). If you eventually want your dog to stay in place until you release him, well then, you need to ensure he maintains his stay until you've released him. Say your release word in a relatively quiet voice. Don't praise and make a fuss when he gets up. You want the "staying in place" part to be the most fun, not the release. This sounds easy, but is harder to do than you might think, so pay careful attention to your own behavior during this process.

Spend several weeks doing these ultra short stays, 2 or 3 at a time, scattered throughout your day, and in lots of different locations. Avoid practicing when there are environmental distractions right now—that's just too hard for a young puppy at this age. You can work on increasing the amount of time you ask your pup to stay, but avoid situations in which it would be hard for him to succeed.

Work on one-second stays, then two and three second ones, but don't go too far too fast. It may take weeks or even months to build up to 15 seconds in a quiet room with no distractions. That's fine, go at your puppy's pace. Patience! The two most common mistakes that people make when teaching stay are 1) expecting too much of a young dog and 2) telling their dog to stay, forgetting to release him and teaching their dog that it's fine to get up when he feels like it.

Throw out expectations of how fast your puppy should progress, and don't try to increase the time you ask your pup to stay in place until you would bet ten dollars he'll succeed the next time you try. Your job right now is NOT to achieve an impressive stay, it is to teach your puppy the beginnings of a fun, new game. You want that sweet, little brain to think "Oh, I get it! If I plant my bottom on the ground, I can get my owner to give me a treat! Sweet!" As he gets older you can begin to ask for "real" stays of a longer duration in quiet environments, or shorter ones when he's distracted by activities going on around him.

WALKING BY YOUR SIDE ON CUE

Once your pup attempts to follow you and settles into the heel position by your side, it's time to introduce the cue. Begin as usual, but this time say "This Way" or "Let's Go" as you walk away from your pup. Only go a few feet, and treat generously any time that your dog is by your side, moving in the same direction as you. You can use the treat in your hand to keep him walking beside you, but guard against holding your hand out as if you were holding a carrot to lure a donkey forward. Work on raising your arm whenever you can so that he doesn't become dependent on seeing your hand in front of his face, but don't hesitate to pop treats in his mouth often to keep him happy to be by your side.

Gradually increase the time between treats, but go back to lots of treats if there are distractions that make walking beside you difficult for your pup. Interweave short sessions of heeling into long, casual walks with a harness or head collar. Be thoughtful about where and when you ask him to heel—don't ask him to inhibit his impulses when you know it's going to be difficult for him. You can start asking for more precision and using a more formal "Heel" cue as he gets older and you are working on "Intermediate" exercises. Gradually you can start pushing the envelope, but a solid heel in a distracting environment can easily take a year or two of practice and experience, so keep your expectations realistic and create as many "wins" for him as you can at this stage of life.

> *Go back to giving lots of treats if there are distractions that make walking beside you difficult.*

WHAT'S NEXT?

Congratulations! You are well on your way to a happy, well-mannered family dog. Did you notice we said "on your way?" If you've gotten this far, you've already made great strides, but your puppy is still a puppy. You wouldn't pull your child out of school in 3rd grade, would you? Dogs aren't fully mature until they are three years old, and it's neither fair nor realistic to expect them to behave like a grown up, fully-trained dog when they are still youngsters.

It is easy to be seduced by a responsive adolescent dog, especially when they have grown so much in size and look more like an adult than a puppy. But raising a puppy means helping them behave responsively until it becomes an ingrained habit in a variety of situations, and that can take a lot of time. That's okay, because "training," if you know how to do it, is just another wonderful way to interact with your dog. So don't stop here—take more classes, practice a little bit every day, and continue to be aware of how your own behavior influences that of your dog. Once you know the basics, and have realistic expectations, raising a dog is a joy. Surely it has some low moments, you can count on that, but what relationship doesn't?

A PUPPY PRIMER SUMMARY

• "Socialization" is important throughout the first year of a dog's life. Loosely applied, it means exposing dogs to a variety of people, dogs and circumstances in a positive, enjoyable manner.

• "Proofing through distractions" is the most important and time consuming part of training. For example, your next step of Stay training might be to ask your pup to stay for 15 seconds in a room with no distractions, but only a one second stay if there is something competing for her attention.

• The biggest mistake people make in teaching any exercise is to jump from step 1 to step 25. Your pup needs all the steps in between, just as you did when you learned a new skill that required concentration and maturity. It can take 2 years to get a solid off-leash recall in the face of major distractions. Asking your pup to sit and stay at the front door when guests arrive is like astrophysics to your puppy—don't expect graduate work out of a first grader!

• Training classes can be a wonderful way to get coaching yourself on your own training skills (yes, it really IS all about you!). They also get your dog out and about, provide important mental and physical stimulation, (and often allow you to feel grateful that you are not the worst dog/owner pair in the class!). However, some dogs don't do well in a class environment, and that's okay too. One of Patricia's Border Collies was completely overwhelmed by all the dogs in an indoor class, so she worked with him in an outdoor class on the other side of the fence from the rest of the group. Don't hesitate to ask professionals what they think is best for your dog. If they are good, they'll be straight with you and help you find the right course of action. However, if their advice goes against your deepest instincts, listen carefully to that little voice inside. If someone is advising a course of action that doesn't feel right, get a second opinion from another professional.

• Read more books, watch videos, and/or go to training and behavior seminars. The more you learn about how your dog *thinks, learns* and *communicates*, the more joyful your relationship will be. Your pup's entire nervous system is geared for learning right now—take advantage of it while she's still young! Remember that involving her in family activities and allowing her more freedom comes from training: It comes from actively raising her to be the dog you want her to be.

• Most importantly, remember that YOU are the one with the most influence on what your pup learns. Although it may not feel like it much of the time, your actions have a profound effect on her behavior. She can learn that she should never potty in front of you on a walk and develop housetraining problems (because you yelled at her for going in the house), OR she can learn that urinating outside gets her a treat. She can learn that it's fun to come when called, OR she can learn to run away from you when you try to call her in from the backyard. Your choice!

• As much as you've already learned from this book and from past experience, don't ever hesitate to get advice and coaching from trainers or behaviorists. They have a lot of knowledge and experience that can make life easier for you and your dog in the future.

In closing, remember to think of training as a fun way to interact with your dog. Work together to improve each of her skills gradually, using a variety of reinforcements in a variety of places. The effort that you put in now is an investment that will pay dividends long into the future. So, off you go now. . . we leave you with our best wishes for a long and happy life with your new best friend.

ACKNOWLEDGEMENTS

Special thanks to Aimee Moore, co-author of *Family Friendly Dog Training*, whose research, experience and collaboration with Patricia has led to some of the best class curricula in the country. She is now the owner of Dog's Best Friend LLC in Madison, Wisconsin, and continues to offer progressive, positive-based classes at every level. We also thank readers who provided us with invaluable feedback of earlier versions, including James Billings, Aimee Moore, Denise Swedlund and Chelse Wagner. Karen London deserves special thanks for her wise and constructive editing suggestions. Several instructors responded to Patricia's query on her blog about what they'd like to see in a new book, and we thank Khris Erickson, Janet Miller, Valerie Olszyk and Wendy Whitelam for their excellent ideas. And a final and heartfelt thank you to Terry Ryan who wrote a book titled *Puppy Primer* in 1990. We stand proudly in her footsteps and those of dozens of professionals around the country. And finally, Patricia thanks all her dogs, from Fudge to Willie, for all they have taught her—and for doing a great job at keeping her humble.

Brenda would like to thank her co-author Patricia for the opportunity she had to work with her and learn about dog behavior from her. She'd like to thank "Kato" for demonstrating vividly to her that all puppies are not alike! Kato taught Brenda that each puppy is an individual with a unique set of needs. Finally, Brenda offers thanks to the thousands of puppies and their owners she has had the privilege to work with over the years, and to those she has yet to meet. Each puppy and their family teach her as much as she teaches them.

Available at www.patriciamcconnell.com

🐾 *The Other End of the Leash*

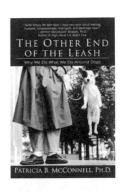

A combination of science and soul, *The Other End of the Leash* explains why we get along so well with dogs, and yet why we so often miscommunicate. Adult primates and adult dogs love to play, but we greet each other and express affection in very different ways. We humans love to hug—as an expression of love or comfort—while dogs see it as an assertive desire to control. (Note: Golden Retrievers have not read this chapter.)

Through a critically-acclaimed combination of heart warming stories and accessible science, readers will come away with an entirely new perspective on their relationship with their dogs.

🐾 *Family Friendly Dog Training*

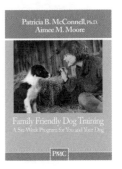

This six-week program for dogs five months and older will have your dog listening to you in no time!

Let Patricia McConnell's years of experience and expertise show you how to make basic training fun, fast and easy.

Equally useful as an adjunct to training classes, or for people who are "home schooling," *Family Friendly Dog Training* will help you connect with your best friend in a way that will enrich your relationship for years to come.

🐾 *Way to Go*

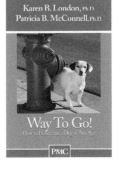

When you hear "housetraining," you might automatically think "puppy," but that's not always the case. Sometimes adult dogs need a refresher course due to age, health conditions, or new environments.

This concise 23 page booklet includes: The importance of management, why dogs go where they go, when a puppy is most likely to need to pee, realistic expectations, and what to do about regressions.

🐾 *Love Has No Age Limit*

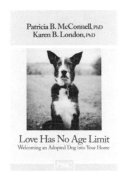

Bringing home an adolescent or mature dog can be an adventure, and you can count on Patricia McConnell and Karen London to be with you every step of the way. Included are sections on preventing common behavioral problems such as separation anxiety, house training, fear-based behavior and trouble between dogs.

Dog lovers all over the country are buying this useful and engaging booklet in bulk, and donating copies to their local shelters to send home with newly adopted dogs.

ADDITIONAL
RESOURCES

PATRICIA McCONNELL, PH.D.

Your source for science and soul in dog training and behavior

www.patriciamcconnell.com/store

Patricia's books, booklets, and DVDs are used by thousands of professionals all over the world because they are clear, user-friendly and employ positive dog training methods. Topics range from teaching a dog to come when called and walking politely on a leash, to treating serious behavior problems such as aggression or separation anxiety. Special pricing is available for bulk purchases.

www.patriciamcconnell.com/learning-center

Walk right in, get comfy and savor a free and comprehensive compilation of articles, blogs and videos about canine behavior and dog training. This is a great resource for anyone who loves dogs!

www.theeducationofwill.com

Interweaving enlightening stories of her clients' dogs with tales of her deepening bond with Will, Patricia describes her efforts to recover from her traumatic past. Hopeful and inspiring, the redemptive message of her journey reminds us that, "while trauma changes our brains, and the past casts a long shadow, healing for both people and dogs is possible through hard work, compassion, and mutual devotion".

Follow Patricia on Social Media

🐦 twitter.com/McConnellWrites

f www.facebook.com/PatriciaMcConnellPhD

▶ www.youtube.com/user/PatriciaMcConnell

📷 instagram.com/PatriciaMcConnellPhD

TRISHA'S BLOG
The Other End of the Leash

Welcome to an internationally-acclaimed inquiry into the behavior of dogs and the people who love them. Trisha's topics include:

- fun and effective training suggestions
- behavior problem solving
- the latest research on animal behavior

- book reviews
- the always-popular "Meanwhile, back on the farm" updates

Sign up and enjoy this valuable resource, which includes insightful comments from dog lovers around the world.

www.patriciamcconnell.com/theotherendoftheleash

JOIN THE PACK!

Join the Pack and receive newsletters about special promotions, sales and Trisha's speaking engagements. Stay informed about new research on animal behavior, not to mention the world's most complicated animals (us!). You will also receive information on upcoming events, and anything else our dogs and cats encourage us to add.

Rest assured, your privacy is of utmost importance to us. We will never sell, borrow, or give away your information and you can unsubscribe any time you'd like.

www.patriciamcconnell.com/join-the-pack

SAVE ON YOUR NEXT PURCHASE

Email support@patriciamcconnell.com with **"Puppy Primer CC"** in the subject line and we'll sign you up for our newsletter and give you a **25% off coupon** on your next purchase of any items on our website.